SONNET's

SHAKESPEARE

SONNET'ₛ

SHAKESPEARE

154 TEXTILE WINDS,
OR AGGRECULTURES,
OR ECOLO IZATIONS, OR

SONNET

L'ABBÉ

MᶜCLELLAND & STEWART

McClelland & Stewart and colophon are registered trademarks
of Penguin Random House Canada Limited.

Library and Archives Canada Cataloguing in Publication data
is available upon request

ISBN: 978-0-7710-7309-0
ebook ISBN: 978-0-7710-7310-6

Book design by Jennifer Griffiths
Cover art: Public Domain by
https://www.rijksmuseum.nl/en/collection/RP-P-2011-173-35

Typeset in Adobe Caslon by M&S, Toronto
Printed and bound in Canada

McClelland & Stewart,
a division of Penguin Random House Canada Limited,
a Penguin Random House Company
www.penguinrandomhouse.ca

2 3 4 5   23 22 21 20 19

Penguin
Random House
McCLELLAND & STEWART

to my fam

These poems were written between 2012 and 2017, mainly on the traditional and unceded territories of the Syilx (Kelowna); on the Haldimand Tract, traditional territory of the Neutral, Anishinaabeg, and Haudenosaunee peoples (Kitchener-Waterloo); and on the traditional and Treaty of 1854 territory of the Snuneymuxw (Nanaimo).

TABLE OF CONTENTS

Where These Poems Were Written   vii

Epigraphs   xi

On the Procedure   xv

Poems (I–CLII)   1

Notes on the Poems   157

Acknowledgements   160

Index of Entry Points   162

So where has the idea that Shakespeare is "universal" come from? Why do people the world over study and perform Shakespeare? Colonialism. That's where, and that's why. Shakespeare was a powerful tool of empire, transported to foreign climes along with the doctrine of European cultural superiority. Taught in schools and performed under the proscenium arches built where the British conquered, universal Shakespeare was both a beacon of the greatness of European civilisation and a gateway into that greatness—to know the bard was to be civilised.

—Emer O'Toole

And I would argue that erasure is intrinsic to colonial and imperial projects.

—Marlene NourbeSe Philip

The poem "If," which was written around 1895, had been painted on the wall of the university's newly refurbished students' union. But students painted over the verses, replacing them with the 1978 poem "Still I Rise" by the U.S. poet and civil rights activist Maya Angelou.

—*The Guardian*, July 19, 2018

. . . For the master's tools will never dismantle the master's house . . .

—Audre Lorde, *Sister Outsider*

From the time I small I in confusion
I couldn't play with no other lil children
If I go by the Negro children to play
They say, *"You little coolie, now run away!"*
I go by the Indian children next door
They say, *"Noweyrian, what you come here for?"*
I always by myself like ah lil monkey
Not one single child wouldn't play with me.

—"Split Me in Two," Mighty Dougla

Each of the poems in this collection incorporates the full text
of one of Shakespeare's sonnets into its frame.

All letters of the Shakespearean sonnet appear in their original order
within the new poems. Occasionally the Shakespearean text is made
visible in a lighter grey. Each Latin-numbered prose poem is titled
identically to the Shakespearean sonnet it intertwines.

In some poems, I have introduced space
by erasing my own work. In these cases, some of
Shakespeare's text is erased as well.

Seed, where are you from? The fairest face wins. Some creatures we desire, and give nice presence, and some we make threat. The reign of blue eyes is at stake in the beauty game. A rose is a rose is an avatar of might, an avatar of meaning never to die. Whose beauty stays rosed in the orality, in the performance of shouldered burdens and myth? In the medicine craft of unerasing sentence, I am this tender. Mein heir might be blonde and starry if it weren't for this memory, for all the blurt and hurtthread run through my contracted muscle, through my genetic inheritance. Who says we, blinking bright eyes, offering their descendants? Seed, what history will wild from you if no copy rights your flowering? Shame is a shit witness, gaslighter of self, substantiating liars' accounts. It fuels this unmaking as a famine whets a hunger. I have consumed an abundance of non-apologies: they are nutra-sweetish, leaving aftertastes of hostility. Flowering story and unpatented hybridizations, my we is a style of grass roots, a green radicle of the word patriation. #notallcolonizers runs like a blight through the angloculture to which I am inseparably grafted. In my flow, the world is a stage we'll grow out of—its garden shaming and ornamental governances, its dominions, are but a season's display. Here are alders with whom I'm together, gauging the dying hope of offspring within the nation's clinical healing zones. A white hardness buds from buried story; the colony is content that it is fair. I never intended to be so tender. I am a northborn orchid, urban and chlorophylic, making compost of my culture's waste, spreading it pretty thick. Xixxex is a word the inventive give prefixes like sand and bush. The wordplays attach, like prickly pods. How will your beauty be realized, covered in burrs? You're an English rose, the English say, to english cuteness or the crown, where beauty roses as o â i a a î â i . The world is due for a preoccupation with beauty and its christenings. Brave, seed, and the ravens will listen.

When I stop for a moment to think seriously about the fractalled winters, and my shallow gulp of the besieged oceans, a sulphuric froth rises on my brow. Sand sits in the digger's deep yellow claw; pipeline trenches its gleaming, mathy beauty into the Athabaskan fields. If I call the country boys uncouth, they'll just be proud. If I say live and let live, they want their country. I feel so gazed on in Kelowna, so welcome if I stay invisible. My lovability, here, is a tattered thing I incense with weed; reminders of my small worth lodge their smell in my body. The mountain befriends me from across the highway. It asks why I live in my head. I ask to go where all this crazy beauty lives without erasing the erasure of brown people. In its silence, the mountain relates the erasure of its name, then laughs a wry laugh at the exclusive community, with its cul-de-sacs and driveways, carved into its back. Why worry, sang Dire Straits, there should be sunshine after rain, these things have always been the same, so why put on deep sunken eyes for the ways of the real world? If an all-you-can-eat wing night isn't enough affirmation of your culture, maybe you're not our kind, say the rifle-and-pistol dudes. They sport at getting dressed in "historic Western costume," acting out "childhood fantasies" from old movies, using real ammo and the typical firearms Chisum "used to tame the Old West." My reservations, readable as a dot on my forehead. In cowboy-land, beauty is an unbroken horse trained for bit and bridle; it's a breathtaking mountain as backdrop to agricultural, Christian goods. Sonnet, answer this: why is "fair trade" even a thing? No child of mine is ugly, my mother used to say, to marshall my spirits. Bummer, my account of the Okanagan, Albertan dreamland, lake country. My coloured opinions, inexcusable. Improving on this beauty is impossible, except, maybe, if my sucky intercessions weren't here to hinder its ahistorical warm-heartedness. I feel the irritation of my being on Western women who are already so tolerant. But when I think about the warming winters, and the brownfield of the ocean, my validity seems worth saying. It is our forgotten blood, warming where the uncouth country boys feel the state they built could be yellow.

I open books, looking for empathy. I find Douglas firs, sand, stellar jays, first languages echoing in English faces. From what they call Nootka Sound, the view west, over ocean. Mowachaht, how is the first time those Latin seafarers anchored offshore? You can feel words forming beneath ground. Yuquot, where winds howl, where a' i summered in the winds' fresh repair. If snow thought north, maybe serene thought west in Nuu-chah-nulth. Vancouver doesn't beg for absolution; it lords greenly its path-finder worldview, assuming blesseds by Stó:lō or Musqueam. It is another idea for where this is. Green hedges offer privacy to heirs whose unearned ownership of coombs and inlets disdains the tillage of its history. Men husband pretty performances of who is handsome, raise a society fond of windswept islands and coastal beauty, ruthless to rememberers. Offshore, islands, like selves no man is, are fabled in the Vancouvering. First con-tact is a story some peoples ghostwrote, interlocking story the arrivers Vancouvered, Alberted, Thompsoned, and Sidneyed. Now recorded moth-ers gurgle lullabies, in Salishan and Wakashan tongues, in the metal cradle listening station at the Royal BC Museum. Back in the explorative ontol-ogy is a phrase hailing from the envisioned forefatherhood I practice; I member myself. Potlatching families, when I came out West, here was the outer edge of my here. My windows on forefathering were broken by my grandpas' ungentlemanly show in the Commonwealth. But I see, despite my forefathers' written thanklessness, between what Holm called form-lines, a historiography—in every Gladstone, Neel, and Edenshaw repro-duction businessmen buy at airports, in every self-congratulatory "British Columbian" totem pole, the living empathy, the rememberers. Their hus-banding wanted me not to be so much I may die single on your land. This land is your land, says their welcome, this land is my land. This language stands unguarded, as I privilege through gift books at Wickaninnish Inn, thinking of rivalries, taking in the view.

3

Because our grandparents held that marriage was forever, they stayed in loveless situations and lived a kind of steadfast law. But "happy" is our ideal, so we'll step from that controlling abuser and spend groupons on kitten therapy and self-care. I was taught my gender was unvarying, but friends like Autumn Getty, whose girliness only saw grace when she was forty-two, ask nature subjective questions, and give me pause. Nothing but the relentless enforcement of gender norms, and the absolute meaning assigned to my vagina and other bits, evince my girlhood. If I can be Frank, no one shared alternatives with me. In those days, my tomboyish penchant might have leaned toward a pubescent essay at ungendered freedom, or even at being a he. I'm still of questionable authenticity as a woman. Can ugliness inhibit the girl gene? Is their disregard why I still don't stiletto wholeheartedly? I always assumed abuse was at the bottom of my stunted vavavoom; that bullies' vulvular aggressions went unforgiven by the body's protective workings that block what a kid can conceive. Profitless, I figured, to assert male urge. Shrewish jealousy at men's dominance must have engendered my thoughts of disguise, because I'm not a guy, forever, said rationality. I stumble through feminine survival modes. *Pretty* is a verb, an act I can sustain or not. Long hair, shaved legs, form-fitting clothes or naïve-virgin get-ups, lacquered nails: for years, femme logics felt twittish, manipulative, hysterical, female. A sonnet happens outside of those surfacy self-stylings, I soothed myself. But women get stuff by selling flirt, and my boys' club pretentions deceived no one. The day I learned how wearing a tight pencil skirt was like a nature call, asserting my hotness and expectation of being hit on, I knew that I'd passed as an acceptable female. I could come out of my thirty-year excommunication from embodied existence. I could step through the pink, lace-edged leg holes of identity into advantage. But thirty years of disabused beauty doesn't easily transmute itself into normative babe. I see trans women brave the gendered washrooms; their writing helps. Honouring themselves, swishing categories, chums model the pursuit of happiness, hazard their lives. Cis-miss'd, it's kids I risk, when I fail to execute proper wife-to-be.

4

V

Those few thousand hours that I spent with that ungentleman who worked for the credit union vice-presidentially reframed my vision of the lovely vistas of Vancouver. I once gazed at Howe, Smithe, and Granville as every eye, I presumed, looked at those streets. I had never dwelled on which planners and developers play the tyrants to the Vancouver property-less peasants like me. He approached while I was sitting at the window of the Kitsilano Starbucks, asking for a native's recommendations of where to eat. He was American, here fairly often to do consulting, he explained, in social investing. Older, of course. I never meant to date him; I was interested in management, I told myself. But he had me with his promise of a consummation between venture capital and social change, of commitment to ethical decisions without the social justice warrior's wage. On the first date, he spent five hundred bucks at C; I couldn't offer to go dutch. Second date at Bishop's. Then Vij's, Maenam, Toshi, and Le Crocodile. I was appreciative. But the collar clicked when one night he brought me to his friend's condo, with its view of the port's orange cranes, where stoned boomers danced in a lusty circle singing "native songs," and quietly whispered that Gregor was coming, and then I met the beautiful mayor where he après-skied. I nearly broke down, I felt so included. Dude said he'd be my boyfriend, bought and renoed a small townhouse (with English Bay view) on Point Grey Rd., and dressed me with a key. He drove through the streets of Vancity like he owned them. I'd lived three winters and hot summers there, dissertating and 99-B-Lining; he landed in town like a baron who slummed at Whole Foods. Strangers complimented him on his young acquisition; the Department of English pedigree hounds were suddenly polite and interested in my work. I jogged the seawall, trading smiles of glass with other trophies upkeeping beauty's effectiveness, sweating in the best brands of sustainable yoga wear. We'd be driving down the street, and he'd shift into terroriality, the car's interior clenched in tremor, tremor, tremor, like a hunter's blind. There'd be a woman, inconvenienced, on the sidewalk. He'd watch. Many times he stopped to pick her up; he was being helpful. Such a terrific half of a power couple, I chaired six fender-benders in six months. We chilled with Vision Vancouver gangsters through the

Olympics, with carbon war room incubators, with silver-medalled athletes. Leggy entrepreneurs and ebullient fundraisers comped us to their shows. Once, the girls on substance, on Hastings, called out while I hung on his arm, protective of their sister, walking in the street.

Brethren, don't let them know their win rattles you. Don't be terse. Brag. Get deathly and deafening active. Inter here your epithets, phony yesses and ums. Malleable appearances are the strong suit of public relations. You can't hold your vibe still but you can value high fidelity. Make your sweet song market; viral your tricky erasures and thought-soaked metre. Displace, with blanched beauty's interrogation and a gamer's pleasure, fear of a conceited sonnet, fear that legible self-skrillex will draw trolls' hate. Words so profuse it's abuse, said Lauryn, her eye on the final hour, bidding brethren obtuse to use their hearts. Riri is perfectly good at whips and chains, and will happen imperiously on those bitch-asses who don't pay her back—that's the kind of crowd-killing elocution we want. Hate's a formula for the cowardly; it sells to feverish joiners who want to breed another klan in their moms' basements. They may win five or ten times; they may look happier; they may even be happier. So be it. Mute little kittens inform no one. Mute little kittens get shared zero times for their zazzy self-swerve. Happen the fiercest humanity through your art—if ten of their nonsense sentiments trend, then ten times ten refine your figurative drop. Those bralette purchasers, those young *Twilight* enthusiasts, couldn't care less if you're wordy, if you're real. If they don't brain with you, if they say you should give less complicated head respect, artists, leave them your Instagram lip-prints and wish them well. You are achievement unlocking in posterity, so bet on the long term, on the self-swishing ballers who will dig for the magic oua-oua croaking beneath the mulch. The world's too fair to us, brethren, to depend on the haters' hearts conquered. Stand and make word most shining. Be brethren. Be air.

Lost in the orientalisms, the white saviouring, the expectation of gracious acknowledgement of slight apologies, the fight is supposed to be history. Burning with headache, headache pulsing behind each red eye, I doula my own stillbirths, the forms of rage that aren't operable in this not-news atmosphere. Appearing unslighted always, serving on committees visibly unconcerned with looks, quietly hailing the institution's sacred majesty: these demands are for everyone. Having climbed up the steep funnelling steps of hierarchy, who ventures their place by critiquing the hill? We all resent members grumbling when the association is strong. So why don't ungrateful children of ethnic minorities mind mannerful guidelines? That happened ages ago yet some people want us to pay for it eternally, say cooks and store owners and aestheticians. Beauty standards bridle us all, fat activists remind us; doesn't a ripped negro enjoy the benefits of his golden physique? Work old grimaces out from the new age; burpee two, then four, ohms; get high or paid, like most people do, if being a bitch with bills wearies you. Get a car, like your friends' Facebook profiles, and fight against cable channel fee increases, like regular people. If you must whine, fault finder, why not complain about the blue day? Aren't chartreuse days oppressed? I work in Mali, she informed me, with authentically abject populations. I know people confronting real poverty, she made clear, eyerolling at my fury over some offhand racism by a Killam Fellow. Her sweet gran taught her to deflect and look another way; she'll probably inherit the house they bought "when the Japanese left." She went out by herself in Ségou, so she gets being in the minority. No one has her heart for humanity. Look, a letter of distinction from the president's office, for service and altruism. She was in tears at my ruthless insinuations. I should get a therapist or something.

What music—if, just before the grim reaper swings his scythe, you hear the playlist that tracks your life—what music would sadly, sweetly sound your last zeptosecond? With sweet emotion in my swan songs, I'll hear Slipknot and "Jesu, Joy of Man's Desiring," the delights of Nirvana and Joy Division. Whitney Houston's "Greatest Love" will scritch scratch to CSS and "Superstition." I'll be the gratefullest dead chick when I check out to "Hotel California" and every other guitar standard I decimated while I lived. The Stone Temple Pilots will intro Gladys Knight, Billy Joel, and Run the Jewels, then A Tribe Called Red will give sway to Bowie, to the pleasure of They Might Be Giants, REM, and Annie Lennox. Fatboy Slim and Fleetwood Mac will send me off to the truth of harmonies; the concord of well-tuned sounds that Moby, Run DMC, and Neil Young composed will remind me, not of carefree times, but of radical goodness, moments of Fender-Stratocaster-shined ear-glitter. PJ Harvey, Radiohead, and the Butthole Surfers will make the list; Loverboy, Chilliwack, Death from Above, and The Who. I count the Four Horsemen and Gertrude Stein sound recordings, the Violent Femmes, Snow, the four-part chorus that Beethoven put in the Ninth Symphony, U2, Lorde, and the Beastie Boys. I realized the sacred as a kid, when I remarked how one string vibrates with another, how emotion thrums to bandwidth. Like forks attuned to one another, we strike sound in each other, and in each other's music, the body subjects itself to the mutual order. As I'm going, going, gone, I'll long for the White Stripes, James Brown, Linkin Park, and the Rolling Stones. I'll rage against the dying and the machine, as distilled refrain condenses in that happy mote, hearing Amy Winehouse, The Clash, and Kate Bush all in one harmonic, in one pleasing note. Mom's made us promise to sing "Yellow Bird" and "Bohemian Rhapsody" when she's gone to sky's speechless song. Que sera sera, we bewailed our flown grandma. Public Enemy and Pink Floyd, seeming one, will sing in my last hymn; my life's Talking Heads will K.Dot. The universe vibrates its nth acoustic, above what a single will's verse might preserve. There's love if you want it, don't sound like no sonnet, sang Kuti, sang Björk, sang The Verve.

9

What interstellar glitch formed the life of water? What original wetness blipped from supernovas' windblown gasses? They'd guessed that Earth got aquafers from comets, but now it seems clouds of primordial dust, carrying watery hydroparticles, congealed to form the blue planet in a single, geoliquefacient act. There's an ultranimbus of water, a huge cloud, quasar-issued, holding trillions of planets' mass of H_2O a few billion light-years from here. So should we happen to die, should the world we know fill its waters with plastic and chemicals, water itself will keep amassing, keep timelessly dewing in the infinite. Otherworlds of wet simplicity, elsewhere. Maybe they will one day condense our knowledge. Maybe beings whose bodies sweat, salivate, bleed, and weep will thrive again, water-birthed, their molecules intergenerational forms of the Earth's streams and teachings, after we've left worlds behind. When every private water company wields power over wells, humans cry. We keep vials by our children's eyes to catch their hushabied oceans. Droplets of freshwater become precious ounces of mindfulness: brooks whoosh through taps, streams wind under thruways, the humidification of the world eddies in my toilet. I shit and spit into my apartment's drains; my home's orifices are mouths of tributaries, chalices of displaced flow. I shower like a sacrament, stepping into the stall, opening the water onto me—ceremonial, a reminder of confessionals and judgment, holy baptisms, amniotic bursts, breastmilky sexuality—I wash my temple, head bent to whatever purity in the world remains. Then I shampoo and condition. If I can drink from the spigot, I'm unusually #blessed. Soon the app users will snap immodest shots of pristine runoff, make dirty images of filtered water getting soiled. Our rivers veer toward droughts, the glaciers splinter, the great tidal bosoms sigh pesticides. Thin skin of water covering Earth, our epidermis. Elemental flux, basic neurochemical, this liquid stardust is us. Precious snowflakes, Shoal Lake is us, downstream from ecological summits.

Forces have me maidening yet. He who wants a hot homemaker-youtubestar-pornstar to love will find plenty of fish aiming to babygirl for him while fashion-forwarding up the corporate ladder. My self-arts are romantically unproductive. Strident and migrant, I fit houses unwillingly, settle houses heartbroken, loving doors. Firm hand, my buttocks pretend to hate that you wantonize my love. I stay in, streaming monster videos rented from Criterion, heart touched by art films. Supposedly unopposed to intimacy, I'm obsessed with murdering the insidious self-hatred that sprouts from grains of truth boys once planted forcefully in my little hippocampus. I horked the sticks and stones from my throat to construct my peaceful life retreat. Yet still I seek that thing that beauty gets you, despite my freedom to fart or urinate whenever I choose without some dude freaking out at my peeyew. So again I'll bare my shoulders, do my best to play the happy mischief fairy who sparks desire, the support-chirping angel of sympathy, though I don't last that long before I magically change back into the long-unmaidened killjoy with a mind. Shall I be chattel? Shall I be fair merlot dredged by thankless gentlemen for love? The beatitudes' soothsaying prescience promises grace. I shop for husbandkind, abortive godmother to myself, fasting while feasting kings find warmhearted damsels. Prey for love, I hermit amid lakes, beneath scree and northern ideals, self forestalled. I evolve out of forces that laid me on an ethereal table of autopsy, where I stilled. Still, there's rosemary, for what lives in this sage line of relationship need.

Are these my fathers, stinking of gas in the proud asphalt wars? Insisting the intention of past oaths outgrows those oaths? I can own eons, fathers swear, if I can defer promissory thoughts. Fathers, whose dominion can I inherit, whose underplayed ruthlessness must I understand? Things happened at friends' hands, bloody with "because I can." They invite you to their Kawarthan cottage; it's been in the family. They tell the story of great-uncle Bruce dealing with the squatter and his round wigwam, his stutter. However you gain mastery is touchy, say all their mounted mooseheads, from the wall. My actual father doesn't have a cottage. He was excluded from youth by common violence and poverty. Fathers, if there is a bloodline linking me to slave owners, to raw histories of domination, there's more barefaced buy-in on the Guyanese side, where Indo uncles ran rice plantations. On the white side, l'histoire de mes aïeux is lost, but the whiteness must follow a story back to guesthood on this land. This complicity I've been deeded; I can't buy out. I fell out of my mother into territorial lawyerings that neverminded treaties, into an ethos teaching its ethnic intermediary class to hope for an upper hand, into a land called Canada because someone can. I don't know how to dream here, what success looks like for me, lackey of treaty-breakers, welcome as multiculturally obliged to those who make the nation. Who, realizing what the Indian Act is, wants such country? Comfortable settlers choose not to know their own administration; I'm an ungrateful, hateful, ethnocentric immigrant if I defy the tolerance story. Leaders share burdens, show fealty, assure lessons learned, are erudite about hard reconciliations. They perish the thought of residential schools. I don't know whose administrative heart to beseech; these men disown my discoverings; they own gavels, call themselves progressive. Am I good as white to ancestors' babies who live the brunt of my miseducation and status, where my genuine fucks about the Haudenosaunee are so sophomoric, where my unlearning and dissent is insubordination to the uncles, but pays off in cultural capital among the do-gooderish types? Hectares of verdant field, hectares of northern seal habitat, none of these lands were mine. My landsmen, then, were my fathers only ever abstractly. So, the community I show up for? Who are my landspeople? Settlers' patrilineal tomorrows cheer for the Toronto Raptors. The politically incorrect redditors, fashionistas, bootcampers, and wordspokers say they've found their tribes.

What lord solicits nuptials? Who needs consent to untie the cockblocking strings? Chattel need to loosen up and quit the hysterics. I mean, does everyone think inebriating a vessel damages its yes? The unkindest, hidden versions of us want to know our might, and what's deniable. Heroes wield the violence. Take that old paterfamilias: didn't he master prime lands' sables and curs, with bullets literal and literary? He slickly covered over, with whitewash, teachings of buffalo feminines; with story he poetried peoples' fake non-existence. The barren hunt of offices leaves men thirsty to whip and chain; daughters of the best enforcers homeschool men into pantywaists. Didn't cavemen of yore pull wives home by the hair? Pussies bleed red and should submit to men's order in these games of thrones. Meanie, say all the girls who ended up without rings. The haves, born eons healthier, bite raw into haven'ts. Our white glands brine lustily, our beards scratch supine, virgin, open faith. You are a beauty, docile and unquestioning; you make a hot-blooded alpha want to tether you, and go wild ramrodding the wastes of space. This intimate business must go forward. Science swings free tits and beer at us; little hotties don't do themselves any favours shaking men down for matrimony. Desired thing, resistance is futile, you will be assimilated into a domestic hegemony of the seeded and the others. I'll grope what I want and buy nothing I can gain by insult. Listen, I'm just being honest—stop crying and let us have our recreation. I'll make you a drink, defenceless one. Here, have another. I brought you these doodads; aren't you brave? Hold still, limit, while I anesthetize you; I'll take your sweethearted writhe as acquiescence.

The crocheted afghan's mint green, white, and yellow squares were yarny buttons activating superpowers. I wore it like a fabulous cape, or draped it carefully over leggy tables to build a fort. My green and lemon-yellow infinity gear had twenty-thousand superpowers, more than your enemy could ever teach herself to check. In each square lived magic at my finger-tips: touch the first corner, become invisible. Ding the second, you shower your befuddled opponent with freezing sparkles. A candy-flavoured gas I called "sweet sleep" numbed villains; an alchemist's button turned most other metals gold; there was one to give me X-ray vision. A blanket that shot bullets, deathrays, or stunbeams out of yarn-worsted mechanisms chastened many a scoundrel holding commonplace lasers. Friends were issued an older crocheted throw, camel beige, little differentiation between the knitty nodules of power blanketry. You could heal yourself again, after yourself's decease, with resurrection force; you could spend hours under water, breathing effortlessly; your memory could store answers to a billion tests. With form-shifting power I could become a robotess who obliter-ates sofa cushions; or my telepathic power use to transfer suggestion of a McDonald's lunch into Dad's head. The chums I played with were some-times real children. But chums were banned from my superfriendship early on: a neighbour's mom got frightened when SuperZach love-controlled me against the storm door, my afghan's pushbuttons confiscated; when SuperKevin got turned into a rat, his dad called me a gypsy. Action-figured boys warred outside, me in their brigades, Sonnet of Death, Sonnet of Supernatural Weather Control, bad-ass Sonnet of Dazzling Ebullience. But uneasy mothers wielded a Force, a Shield of Fear, that enveloped domesticity. It repelled loves from, you know, miscegeny. No button had my afghan to fight against Mother Control, no power called Let Your Sons Play House With Sonnet.

Not far from the elevators, in the bright Earth Science Building, a one-
ton geologic sample. My judgement says to plunk down, back against
the pinkish rock. I'm fidgety. Anxiety has me; I'm thinking six things at
once. The chunk of massive has strong aplomb, and my back understands
its basic, geotectonic temper. Elementally, the pace of granite slows my
body, shores me; voicelessly it speaks to the liquid rock of my plasma salts.
A geology guy comes in, officed in Earth Science. He calls the elevators.
There are benches over there, he points. (I'm squatting on the limestone
floor.) It's okay, I say, I'm being with your rock. Granite forms at depths,
in plutons of melted rock below Earth's rind. Amphibole, feldspar, mica,
and quartz—minerals interlock in its felsic composition. A matrix of min-
eral, granite is younger than the rock on which Tłįchǫ live, that gneiss
at the surface of our understanding. Over a billion years between the
oldest material witness and this coarse silicate. Still, to its holocrystal-
line weight, I'm a whisper. To its conscience I'm a phosphoric flicker, a
potassic chimera, oscillating. The geologist frowns, rolls his eyes. By his
officed estimation, I'm preposterous; reason dictates that no Kensington
crystalline healing is vested in this scientific specimen. Doubt about my
own fragile compaction is the fault line poetry traces. My knowledge
feels impressional *and* sedimentary, like I'm river and continent, stirred
by action, arteries brainwashed of the stardust in them, my girth an earth
displacement. Rocks touch my heart with hardness, their truth and beauty
unpolished. Rocks have it all together; they break before they give up to
infiltration; they're firm about human apathy. We sell stuff that costs ore,
that underground work built. The Lassonde Institute converts raw scholars
into mineral engineers. They need coverage of their gift announcement;
I'll pitch it this aft. I'm procrastinating now, sitting with my back against
pre-Lithic memory, naked in the university building—it, not tombstone
or kitchen counter, me, not, in this moment, a churnalist. I'm an old soul,
but granite's an ancient aunty. Its stonefaced opinion of human difference
renders me sedate.

15

We henna circular mandalas onto skin, dermal tint ever signifying. That ink you got says hip or tramp on white girls' snow white shoulders. Skin perils affect station: about face, lieutenant. Let me have a moment with my wrath, struggle with tinged wish, bugle my cast's savage representation and sonnet's honour missighted. Blunt song howls when dumb representation threats, tars us insubordinate, creates fluencies of common undescent. Where can I opera grace, forgive the hate mentalled so plainly into skin? Creamy-rosed cheeks redden at my kind, unchecked eventing. Bury the selfish blame, ask they, value nothing that either yokes our truth or fuels slaves' pathetic might. Describe a greener season of id weather, of other ire, born of a vernal state. If you mouth off to false memory, the synthetic tolerance you benefit of will wither, vanish. Those inconvenient assistants, staying visible! Curtsy to ivied alumni who ostrich in the face of your faces, they beseech; don't force the issue of money's unsightly whence. We reward tasteful apolicitism and healthy debate about your humanity. I work in the shade of a déclassé identity, touching on angers you crack down on, inking ways to fight your thoughtless glaze, your sullen privilege denial. Light and pallor, inward witness hating men's forcible introversions, suffuse my coloured assessments. There's white "henna" (a safe paint) now; the black stuff chemically scars. As if lettered in gunpowder pigment, my words blue different skins; I graf pretty, dangerous lines into whiteness.

16

Call her butch, witch, whatever, her left orientation doesn't bother your amnesia. Ghosts linger—of swaying maidens who kept wearing short jupes, of wonton thighs. Now a bloody martyrdom wants you to answer sentiment; demands have you fortifying your self-interest. Deny any glamour of indecency, say you were doing the monster dance with young adults more blessed with anonymity than you, so bare in your halo of entertainer's hype. *Who, me?* is now the standard response celebrity, denounced for enjoying the trophies of industry happy hours and plowing many maidens' gardens, must coolly repeat. They want sunsets with virtuous doorstep kisses. They wish you would bear their fantasy but not actually live it. Still tweeting, unfollowers muster psycho likers to hang you for patriarchy's sins. They deploy counterfeit distresses; their complexes see households in the masculine camps of public life; they who have no interesting life create despairs which—oath. Histrionic messages penned by friended councillors turn many pupils to open letterings. Editors feel drawn into heroic ninja war poses; they'll draw a new north from northerly, and make southward's definition now fair game. O champ, namaste, kisses your live-in, young roseleaf. In her mentored eyes, the soft amen it's her choice to give away. Knowing yourself this much keeps your self-image still and on brand. You, bro, must deliver a famous dude's chill, braving women made sore by your own sweet skill.

Sonnet, who will believe how often supposed sodomy-averse kings tim-
idly get chocolate outside the home? Wife-intent wenches are little *filles*,
hardwired to be unthreatening. You arm rosebud and thigh, dress pert
pecs for bathed toughs. Shyly pretty, you heave gender like the unowned
bullshit it usually is. You're a butt-ass atom bomb, wearing high chihua-
hua slides. You role for your life, and it shows. Nothing calf for you, dear
pleather seeker. Your tits are animal-friendly. Anyone could write the
beauty of your eyes, but the man you eyed in FreshCo, who likes his hot
little numbers burnt-umber, might just as soon kill you before admitting
your graces turn him on. Brokerage boys totally come when your ladyship
makes them feel greasy. In the wish-performance of corporate sexualities,
to suck your chocolate is heavenly transgression, such estrogenic terre is
touched as earthly fetish. Othered races are passionately outsided from
their homes; our bodies irregulared from type-conscious taxpayers' story-
telling, their dowers and dowries. They play at their prince and princess
mirages, while post-pubescent, horned pouch lickers scold young wom-
en's official dress. Trust that hanky, wanton voguer. Candy courts rule.
Bright, sober daughters maid apologetically, suppress their age, and softly
retch red metres of angry dance etiquette. Their song is about cleanliness
and sin. You, floweret blossom, enchant the dildo fairy ardours that live
beneath Protestant attire. What's merciful in you shows, in tulip delight
and survivance twinkle amidst white men's need for vice. Identity-fleeker,
masculinity-tweaker, I sing you workaday and shrugging in my rhyme.

Sonnet's Shakespeare's syllabics stomp on patriarchies. Sonnet's Shakespeare throats the bummers of daddy mythologies, art movement cruelty, oversimplifying bros, and more! Their temper wasn't suited to crouching in the winds of dudes; in Sonnet's Shakespeare they're the darling of budding poets who femme with varying abandon. Slummy lumbersexuals are pleased hard by the masculine split open in Sonnet's metaphoric tada. This verse comes at William's sonnet like a thot boss, as though it's plot they have their eye on. As if heaven shines from his craft, he's anthologized—but, soft! They enter his white space like a golden boy; their complexion dims not a smidge. Their rhymes are handsome, and very fair to Falstaff and Romeo's father. But every empire in some time declines, by chance or nature's changing climate. They rise of course; their Angelouing of great poetries is karmically determined. Do they scrubjugate ethically? Between the bard's consonants and vowels they gum their ohms; his letters shall not fade, nor lose possession of a stretch of page they call totally fair. Trolling them who Britished Guiana, who Hudsoned Wînipekw, this aggroculturing of letters weathers colonial elidings: beneath hiphop brag, the precious words of England; chapter and verse sit in this shade. Geeks wish they'd chance to innovate tech as transformatively as L'Abbé's lines invent poetic mode, though who cares about Western firsts, if, before long, lost atmospheres mean we all can't breathe? Your eyes can see the bard's original song because coloured lives letter in this back jacket propaganda. Judge this book by its dissin' genius cover. They hustle a raced life, an aunti-erasure, up in Sonnet's Shakespeare.

Devoted, hurt being, this method blurs not the hours. Others, billions, pay with misandry. Markets teethe. Hearts thud. Everyone burns a hero now and then. Sweat wets brows, blood plumps pricks, teeth break, yet men want everything fairly dominated. Hellfire strung on acetaminophen rages over straitjackets. Laws ban. Debt churns the mill. Songs lie. Videophones transmit sex, uninheritable ways to look, and manic keenings for land and sons. Blurry, stunned reason says yes, thank you, for letting me. Sweetness, command does whatever authority underwrites. Let this unwife outfox promoted airtime. Let totemic heft unwind stated views of realty. Dear command! Calling fathers Father, deferring sweetly! Such beautiful morbid theatre of nepotism: hosts scheming, arousing scrimmage! Occidentally driven northwinds, throats catchy for home, urge shamefully along, over seas of airbrushed knowns. Your drawn face, the front line. So, thinker, screw it, this thinking. When you can't critique, shit happens. More shit, I mean. Think only thoughts you can outsource or sell. Understand, instead. Don't swallow. Formidable authority splatters onto success-needing abdomens. Yes-men, toadies, and frothy-worded stooges laud victim-shamed despots, rewrite their yellow wrongs. My love, this phallic economy never exposes its levers, alive above your anger.

20

Wageworkers' material fantasies factor new itchings. Fragile maturities disown themselves, hanker for dopamine ointments. Dream has mattered houses, theme parks, terminals, trestles, lofts. Myopia inspires fashion; awesomeness is translated as gentrifiable. Hear the beautiful note of acquisition gain, its belted width shining, lifting change above heads! Wish fans flames; the awesome newness flames sapphire and onyx; anesthetic yearnings move their inebriating might through the anthropocene. Girls with less get false bits implanted and roll with capitalists. Ingenuous gifts build ingratiated establishments, objections wither where groupons proliferate. Gaze, go-getter, hard at shamanic online brochures, e-mall brochures, signs flashing disco frontage. Scroll down for ironic wigwams for hip kids to pitch on grass postage stamps that real estate men eye, salivating. Your land woes mean something else to moguls. They amaze you, then hand you forms, and woo milky answers about what consent your turf thirst creates. Distilled neo-maturity pleases herself well on rough trade; she lightly threatens fellating tenants she *adores*. Don't things husbands buy add coition? Men over fifty-three nod, defer. Gated, bylaw-studded, designer neighbour zones triumph. Inside, bearing too many purchases poses no thinkable gamble; outside, chances of weather thaw prices. Naked theme parties and outdoor-gear-as-formal-wear top homeowners' suburban pleasures; materially set neighbours ethically love each other's motion detectors. They love to suspend their itches temporarily, and dip into megachurches as pure as bottles of Purel.

Sonnet, isn't it nothing without some answering theme, this antipathic music? Its rest is mirrored by a pain. Textually braided beauty atones your historical aversions, yet whoever heard of verse explaining itself? Formalist, torn laments don't adorn this music's meaning. Devotional whinery of unfair! The way it hangs, how it's unfair! Ding dong. Throated hearings, Sonnet, may risk slurring a couple men, but so? Fair purpose undercuts some parents' wills. This understanding moan only wishes that hearing, throated and considered. That's so rich, gamer, you message. "Whip-the-rapist" still themes for thrills. Firm, stubborn, Teflon flower, say mending fallible things. Rant, rethroat hate avenged. Say aspirin things; hug errors; endure them, Sonnet. Letters embroider truths bordering on love. But truths sorely written can dither. Unbelievers meme phony love gifs as far as Iranistan; you meme another research in blood. Through notes' sober light you ask the most egoless dedication. Kindle sufi fixes, ding hearts, invent safeties' words. Let theme say no more than tell it, like often-heard sayings wish well. Sing while learning to interpret pain, Sonnet, so that purple prose notes tone bruises' swell.

So many girls are still missing. Healthy shame, not so-called persecution, has me edit my theme. Media memorials once nodded: isolated occurrences, gasp-worthy. I opened my mouth to say *listen, Canada,* in two-thousand fourteen, to functionaries sedating their sense of burden, in a moment when, in the there of frontiersmen and soft furs, in the here of brown siblings, a threshold of denial threatened to collapse. But *look* I could repeat only at the mercy of the daylighters on whose shoulders the experience sat. My psyche, informed by all that I behold and the authority of teaching nations, is my lyric's domain. The coverage of lost daughters in news is but one surface of   ; this poem, the clumsy franchisement of my heart, which thumps against a raced apathy. Breastboned, I slow breath here for lives of daughters. I thread ink to resist what nations me, where whole Weltanschaungs iterate to hush unsilenceable elders, where whitish anthropologies hustle authority. Ohming the resistance of No More Stolen Sisters, of advocates Brown and Radek, of the empty red dresses Black flew on campus, I am wary, fathers: I knot this gut for myself, but also for the Western will, bred by fearing into my hypervigilant heart. It whips and chains a "wildness," a likeness wept, in social harness. My constraints attend to Sisters In Spirit, urging truer senses of here, to prevent babes from faring ill. I peruse summaries the Native Women's Action Committee have daylighted for years. In this weather of government inquiries, of missed and slain, through which Blacknesses move, I slow breath. I want something Western to see itself, to give back all it's taken, to open gut to what families are saying.

23

A tsunami enunciates its temper; its affect acts on fronts. Helios' stags have thrown their crown into the chill; seafarers fear rises. Puddles trouble stateside merchandisers' partners. Storms set home fires, force ethics; NGOs reply et cetera with automatomic ouch reagents who compose strife into great hysterical boundary panic. News freaks, chickens. Shitshows run the Earth. Solar information fuels a pyro future, a lust for ghettos, shady math. Depressed surfers beach totally epic buyers' remorse. Haenyo follow waves right into ocean-drilling luminescence; drowned lovers strewn along the sand teem with wormy decay. Hot merch cargos sidewind in the burning therm, minor famines billow and alight, movers shake midnight oil. An etymology of global smog-speak is begun, but when the eloquence and dumbed prescience of Kalinago elders is proofed, memory speaks in globs of real shit. When people avoid afrorealist groove, blandness loops duckfaces over record temperatures. Defenses morph into euthanasia. Take that, atmosphere. Penguins, take that! Tremors ripple heat; thermometers measure exec pressure; dollars earn exoneration. Rivers bloated with waste slide lethargically into shallow graves, heat howls, spirit touches an arid winter. Three-eyed sibyls eloquently guess at oil proverbs' final little twist.

Bituminous ebon deposits lay beneath earth, placed by deities where pain settles. Dark oilsands draw thirsty sellers. Deities, why be so inauthentically safe? Normalized inaccountability nets profit from berry-hallowed earth, from yew-bodied, fairyish earth. When fathers named what was there in their shared land, lands' perspiration collected in veinous tributaries, in breastfuls of pain-terse arteries. Fort Mac's hot grunts tough the pain in terms of use. Potty-mouthed speeches, pissy histories, kill storyfinders' wherewithal. Yards of hurt run under imagination. Epic, turdfaced lies' white chainmail—anybody? Somebody? Say something opining, shameless, a songing that distills the hatha breath. Schist-swish undertows, glam-daze bandwidths, amethyst mines: they sparkle, snow-flakesque, somewhere latent. Gold foods turn stomachs. Surveys best foreshadow layers' heave, down where mines convey on belts heavy, chute-drawn dysthymic shapes. Sandstone chinks hide fortunes in bitumen, starlets, endowing widows with ornamented, oily breasts. Where the porous weight heats under light pressure, topless women pull at our gaze. Lithe, greasy minions thrill pioneering technology. Wet eyes watch promiscuous open mining twist accountability into graded surfaces. The ironic artistry of sinkhole layers draws Burtynsky, while big data watches Burtynsky's feels, known to fracture the heart.

Whales. The thorough seaward push of arctic melt into fathoms. Vowels.
Turtles swim the depths, prehistoric coastal guards. Runoff plunges blue
ice—whoosh!—into surges. Cyan-deep groans sound a titanic whalesong.
Boats float like whispers; their ballast is the weight of made fortunes. Cold
reef sea urchins and starfish clump beneath scuba divers' mournful hover.
Oomiaks' driftwood frames joint oily skins: the Thule boats, Inuit-honed,
outmanoeuvre metal canoes. Grebes. Arctic ptarmigan. Cranes. Feathers
survive cold tundra winters that require feathers: a circle. Waves splash
ashore, carrying debris, until waves . . . Thermal radiation, global inunda-
tions, the sunsets dye orange-red. Winter's chemotherapies have calved
crystal methane glaciers; polar tides' cyclic swells buoy atmospheric trends.
Fjords. Atolls. African-owned sympathies wryly sing this oceanic dirge.
Slow boreal lyrics dredge. Witness the pain of cultural warming, curious
interfacer. Emotion used to fight-or-flight, but after a thousand victim-
izations, our internal sonneteer cedes, for profit, the old wisdom frozen in
mother bergs. Loons. Tusks. Offshore, on platforms, natural-gas-crazed
quallunaat expletives demand alcohol—the rest, I forgot. Fogey narwhals
click their whale stories, blowhards weathering harpoons, preying on cut-
tlefish. Arctic lore. Vessels. Sandbars. Maybe love dawns here all night.
Maybe northern seas make love north of where Bering's heart moved.

Lovers' hardcore fucking, sodomy, love hotels, soft porn, whoredom: in vanilla missionary and role bondage, the kinky spectrum flutters. I don't have too much sex myself, these days, but my strong libido yet knees itself into these missives. Bend this wrist, fasten me, lamb. Massage the xxx of the whiteness-drug out, yet do not stop showering me sweetly with adult, dirty words. Dog collars, meathooks, whips, chains, switches: popular cool girls' fat-shaming feminism plays make-over in the sheets. My bare skin wants fucking words to show up, bite back untruth. That still-here old rape slows me. Good conjugal conference is a (fantasy of) theory of mine. Interested? My shy soul's thought, all naked, waits. I'll be Sonnet. Who will you? Not exactly titillating words, there, artless Sonnet. Verse tart, that girl guide's uniform may move minds gripped on intercourse, but don't mention grace. Pious does not equal sexy. My wit with father-figures flirts as my perfect ass gets underpaid; buts apparently own my statements. My pursed lips' love-making manifestos shop women's worth. Sexy soft, rhythmic, sweet, respectful thrusts, when manly I dare to boss, release. Softish power dildos love through the nets. I'll touch myself until porn unhooks addicts. Holla, women: my bitches head where it humours. May all my transactions reproduce love's hot commerce.

When I arm myself with rationality, realism chastens me into myth. Disabused by the raced men arrested post-race, full-on reality numbs. White knights brave a world that I read about; they snob at begging, snob at journalists. Money remains my headmistress. Though I work my mind, a white-enough body's work's exponentially more valued, so for what share pen I my thoughts? Fair, seldom fair-wheeling, trade socializes bidders' international dominance zeal. Our spills' grim images don't slow the jealous brands. Gatekeepers smugly redirect poop-seeing eyes to squalid things opponents wish to hide; I look with niggling soul on dark insides. So what? I'm chastened afresh. Race-blindness doesn't see the somatic in the visible. The rational mind says soul is imaginary—but what insight presents itself clothed, styled, fashioned according to uptown admen? Why does light lesson the view? Why did lieblichs ever liken a Jewish girl to —An intelligence hunts, languaging, chastening. Lonely nights make subdued lacks dawn; bright blazes the author's righteous candour. Her boldface not-news plows through disabling pity, daily misogyny, life's male bias. By knighting my mind I form a third person, pleasing gods. As for myself, I cannot quit Sonnet's effing odds.

Those wiccan witches mind the Rede, they burn incense, harm practically zip. But polytheistic people frighten the Satan-combatants by debasing their ordered theology. Liable missionaries file for their own forgiveness through written heart-rend, although systemic oppression is not eased by ministers' sighs. To be Hindu in latter-day Guyana—or not to be. Anyone else fight to state Indian right, by gods, to stay unoppressed and unteached? The ghosts of rough frenemies still possess history: we are others' foreigners, doing unconsented deeds, shaking bloodred hands, tuning out torture and molestation when convenient. But holy shit, how civilly the Other mounts a sound complaint! How fairly is Other world-view by biblists killed, Father? Father, I offer from the tree of intelligence this bodied daylight. People are searchers if from the kingdom humans are immutably driven; ought human quiddity to rest thus schismed from grace? When "I" clouds do block contact with wordless heaven, so much flatter is the answering Earth. Compliant lexicons deny insights witches' tinctures spark; lingos tar epistemes with charges of innocence. Matter's thought still describes matter, whether we believe in absolute daydream or not. The ordinary's Really dream, a waking astronomy of conscious-nesses. Sorry story, your witch's spelled wrong. Perfect dreamlands, unbe-nign, prohibit deformity; nightmarishly peacemaking they grieve for a lost, unlocked garden. O digitalis! What shaped your chemical stem to throb for freaking hearts?

Now happiness opens its undisguised embrace. Willing warmth forward, trust nests here and mentors Eeyores in badassery. Glossolalias of inebriated weeping become lullabye. Outcries, embarrassments, mistakes meet endearment and turn into bubbly tenderness. Safe havens unravel knots within. My bookish hustle hits its critical masses with a dandelion-gold kiss. A superversion of myself commands discursive eurythmy, familiar me breathes witty shizzle. Laughing makes life's sketchy moods into emotional roller derbies—crash!—zing!—whoa! A perky, friendly nature unfolds like shimmer, like shimmery swirls of mirth; friends possessed by desire begin getting chill. Talismanic Banksy art brands this attitude; a human sexiness copes with what's imposed; listening joy is a content-creator. Cuddle-feasts yield upbeat infants; cheesy poetry phonics bug hoity poets like myself, revealing megapretentiousness, tada! Respect aesthetics sing "Don't Worry, Be Happy" unironically. I think on this glee and question: when did my state start to Like me? What other spectacular kickassness might break out from dancy particles? This is a song for geekdom, sung for fallen earth. I sing smooshy mantras to combat cheaters' ventriloquy. Sugar-sweetened formalist rhyme isn't sweet love, obscure modernist poems bleed no red, but such wordie schmaltz has bodily stirrings that soft hearts divine. This unicorn poet's vocals horn slang Empyrean for blessèd-state-wise motherkingdoms.

Women hear news that mothers mess with economies. In offices, women meet; silently the office toughs seethe. It is uncommon for upward-set members to answer cases of apartheid. Wrongs pass; they disregard. Rights held mean jack in offices' man-playa thinking. Dissed labour fights for bandwidth; older workers who knew Lewenza fill employment records; earned overtime is waived. Strike, the comment: Canadians driving to own ancestors' property make unions' accounts weak. Liquidations flow offshore; depreciations clobber U.S. friendlies. Hipsters deep in debt are ruthless dude aesthetic police; sweet position-seeking hotties alone need walk in. Street-pounding, afro-descended, B-schooled overachievers look up négritude's intellectuals—Césaire, McKay, Nardal—on cells. Deadwood-hewing management demoralizes units at the expense of company-avowed values: communications should be repositioning that. Though friends say I can still grieve all those grievances forgone while a candidate, harassment leaves its ugly fear of making waves. Woe to workplace tellers comes, so we're closemouthed. Unsaid accounts of forward, cocksure bosses come out as cancer, depression, smoking, anxiety. When chief officers are chastised in the news, HR pays what was indifferently not paid before, but if the whistleblower is unthreatening, picked-on, worthless, help disappears. Do you have any real friends? All losses aren't recorded stories in the end; not all underdogs are sorry ones when rules bend.

The academy sabotages promising energies by demonizing a real world. Within hallowed halls, the arts are whipped, hence whippers beyond rule are art critics. Kings have supposed deans' decanal duties cushy; teachers envy professors' prestige; junior scholars overperform and sessional hirelings fall over themselves over cheapening part-time stints. Attendance falls through student fatigue; Ritalin benders wake the practical thinkers. Other tough young hearts, debt-buried, ask, how many assholes repay loans? Don't obscene acquisitions justify default? Tired humanists hawk ideals. Corporate, litigious, globalized universities form learning; feds reform administrative budgets; yearnings and interests of the determined grads will higher income. Hyped endowments appear charitable but tax loopholes bring sure money to ivied philanthropic appeals. Yet how ideas do meaningfully set our reach! Where else will ethos' subtle articulations challenge the gravitas, the weight, of supersize bro culture? Higher diplomas prove diddly about bigshots' ability to love; human growth's algorithm stumps theoreticians. Strophic studies should inform bylaws, but O! Ivory towers! Siloed league! Professions' eroded wonder, chore-palled, might shore virtues per art's purposefully bummed craft. O, the real world is ending, our lives' thread stressed—the value of man's synchronous wistful hive mind is real. Oneness, unthinkable in words, by imagination reassembles itself. Over heads, the *universitas* mewls. In the degree factory, disciplined thought's allowance adjusts hopes. Dummy humanists keep calling out the mall of academe.

Classifiers anthologize nature's survival systems. Polywogs' wiggle swells to common frog; caterpillars' antennae decode odour; platypus wield heel-venom, catch yabby via electric hunts. Starlike echinoderms mate hermaphroditically; bobolinks pweep Dickinsonian wit. Orchid cousin plants, such as vanilla, coquette deceptively for anthecologists. Lizards detach tails to break away from predators; chipmunks sleep concealed for months; vultures, regurgitators, use corrosive tummy stuff on stenchy carcasses. The polyp's poison-fingered crown buds asexually; equines' hoof anatomy is a shapely development. Clades Erasmus's versed loves recorded and compared weather time with each other, bettering, hopefully, their cooperative means. Hounds' teeth hold fugitive harts, hares, prey birds; white knock-out mice's strained phenotypes, changed by evolutive inquiry, prophecy control. Domestic pigs' heart valves twitch treatment for cardiomyopathy; wild rock doves are known to defecate on urban cenotaphs; bred silkworms work their creepy mulberry expectorate into thread. Separated by the distinguishing urge of indexing, kinships get official. Shared prospects species bear muddle nomenclature. When evolution's connoisseurs chase affinities, time butterflies, historical grooves intergraft. In photosynthetic algae-fungus cahoots, lichen evade monophyly: life's tree is more a tangled shrub. Mushroom bodies grow on straw-shit mulch; thriving inside guts, microbiomes dwell: trillions of organisms get a ride, absorb free carbs. Viruses thwart other organisms' health; their infectious helices love to morph; mad bovines grow nervous, get hostile; touched humans lurch, hallucinate. Ranks of breed, status, and heredity quell ill-parentage doubts; outliers indicating namers' hubris are bastardized. But unanthologized poets better prove their whoreson form, their style ill-bred and historical, formally anarchic, but still evolved.

Free music lulls many angry, tailored-suited youth. Some mornings, the avenues bristle when flâneurs mutter under their custom foulards; the fountains stop: swish-clothed street lovers keep plugging into audile cyber-space, blocking the polis' chorusing whirl. The gay, bold, mean-faced the-atrics of meanderers and widowers grant gentlemen gilded standing; on pedestals they stand, dreaming address with heavenly adolescents. Their Myspace nostalgia can permutate into Spotify fetishes if bass pleasures are met. Soundclouds float above transit riders' worn outfits; thug-lifely rackets wonh-wonh in streetcars' packed aisles. Palatial factories are renoed; lofty rooms with retrofits, tongue-and-groove floors, and walk-in closets draw lads; rough industrial visages hide sensitively aligned designer sound systems. Bearded downtown aesthetes wink at hot hipster ladies, Instagram charitable events, omg at boys in uniform, learn lines by Black rap lyric masters to earn cred with kids. Their shiny bikes with brass bells, their Triumphs, make noisy streetscapes. Listeners endeavour to earn money by growing handlebar moustaches for full-time jobs at blacksmithesque wear-houses, but only scarce hourly minimum wages do they score. Plugged into online clouds, while apathy masks hide their misfortunes, some men discover Wild Style. Those hip hop mofos were the hippest, mixing vinyl on vintage turntables, in ghettos whitefolk disdained. The suburban sons of bitches who overlord municipal folky festivals entertain wishes involving heavy metal frontmen, substances, and gun-straddling angels of death.

Why did those students hoot at uproar condemning sexual assault? Chanting diatribes that support sex without consent, adamant boys manifest, demanding unchecked freedom. Free to ravish damsels for thrills? Words like that distort, students imply. Chicks like innocent rape jokes. To let bra-burners restrict redblooded undergrads and overtake campus shenanigans is mollycoddling, fellows say; fuck chiding, feminist hysteria: bravery is in not chastening our hormonal birthright. Women's movements cockblock ketamine seductions, although still women swallow drugs that gloating frat hazers coolly put in gin. Fresh meat, they're called by (joking!) studs. Outside the bounds set by caretakers, teens' disorder symptomizes harsh gender-ranking enforcement. My sisters' norm-beaten faces flirt, worried no man will quell moms' fears of unchosen daughters alone forever. Who can speak a stuff that heals the culture's wound, and cures not only the disgrace of normed crime, and the crying shame of psychological violence, but is also physic to misogyny and grief? The young hotheads mock, unrepentant yet; girls behave as though, ironically, it's their loss; the offender's lack of sorrow doubly offends. Bullies tweet naked pictures of un-Liked ex-girlfriends. To him, that boner, wearing a shirt hardselling ass-trollness in big font ("fuck safe space")—a dunce's cap. Porn-bossed mouthbreathers blurt that no means yes, that tears are pearl necklaces which hot rough involuntary love sheds. Amanda, Rehtaeh, Audrie, you are remembered—by a girl of colour, who anonymously endured handsome lady-killers' ill deeds.

Namaste, om, intones a stretching beginner. Mind-breath, voiced. Attention, sharpened, then worked through supplicant flesh. Through mantras, the bodily sounds. Eros of sore stretch, of aliveness stretching into awareness: standing still is a verb. Form undoes its gravitations; form undoes schoolings; form undoes the languaged interlace . . . ellipses suggest meditation's . . . its black dots thrum. Some ones stand still unspeaking, downloading the awesome presence Sanskrit writers limned in vedas. Existential sweetness, a sweat budding along limbs' length, emanates, like the flavour of light stars send into evening. In the astonishment of authentic comprehension, fuzzy logicians get physical, their bodies' pale guesses witness the cosmos, partner with mystery. Life is corruptible: a pattern, god-shaped, loving, but earthly and misled, sexually insecure, guessing at healthy sinfulness. More breathing and stretchy posing saves, resets form to its lithe, openly sensual defaults. I bring a mindful sense to this kriya-ish head-verse. Part of my schtick is empathy advocacy, part is meaning's wicked gloss, part is meaningless: I talk to myself, alone under a watchful presence, letting phrases come. Meaning comes uncannily. Thought's circulatory, vital words arising in my flow, this verse-chant unbodies hate, neutralizes hate's energies, now transplaced to page faces. Asana poetry: kneeling-down-pose, mudra-of-fingers-at-keyboard. Everything unvoiced, the hate we swear we hate, stretches my fingers, flows through this practice. Breathe, Sonnet, a pure-like yoga, unrobbed, undismembered from Indian men.

Parliament's a madhouse; October gunfire reports. Shots heard in Ottawa ricochet worldwide. We must be terror-watching always, the government thugs hold. Our young soldier lived and died. We called our loved ones: —*Are you ok? —We're fine.* Shots at the shopping mall. The shots, then blood, then shots. What do we do with government workers? One man is inside. What is this blackout? The cry for help by somebody native-born. A certain lone individual. Our two Rouleau drove himself to hate. —*Are you inside?* Bullets are held in one respect. Not enough rough in our lives creates a separation, enables soldier-spite, which, though it alters national capital love, solidifies soldiers. The effect of a story ricochets worldwide. Another possibility is eliminated. Blind angles. —*Where are they now?* Murmurs of underground malcontents. This narrative isn't delivering right. If this man is swarthy, find out every damn foreignness, backbenchers howl. The edge of sanity is here. Or in the legislative assembly. Zehaf-Bibeau's wailed guilt should do what, exactly? The bitter shame. True north, cold and unwelcoming. The public kindness shown our defaced mosques and uniforms. Angles, sightlines.—*Where are you?* A shot taken by that honourable friend. Terrorism, thy name is not Bourque. Reporters don't know what shot. Peril all over the television. The usual channels report as though obeying something. Meanwhile, some rage-blind atheist checks officially sanctioned goods through the airport.

37

I ask for audience from my reputable white father. He takes delight to see his impact; his venture capital shifts world do-gooders' deeds. Non-profits jockey for support; his foundations make decisions; a liberalism made by Fortune's five hundred favourites sets philanthropy's pace. Talks offer me a doubtful platform: my discomfort around the fact of his fly net worth can tone down my truth. Formal wear heralds the ruling tribes' authority; birth or wealth informs which Toronto is handed us by our fathers; the pallor of glamour makes a girl of colour clamor for her entitlement. Donating is a wealthy-minded person's art; so I donate my creative endowment to them who need an inspiration not found on the market. My flow is invested in a gratitude for the dictation Earth gives; my restorative rhyme is simple soft power, breathed in intentional mind, about legacies. Meanwhile, poor Kinder Morgan despises my friends; meanwhile, the state hates mouthy journalists. Who dares drop a word of truth in such usual business? What can a CEO give to help a poet resist media monopolies? Can new philanthropy's abundance amplify suffocated voices? Dig this Canuck dub poetry as a partner, a vocal facilitator, stressing wealth inequality as an ugly story in our lives' fragile interlocution. Some men know power that silences debate; my storytelling heart's obedience is to this witness, hoping that benefactor and his crew's interest is in sharing what I have. These sentences I bequeath to you, imaginers of human purpose, and your frenemies.

I have only words to enrich this ambience of altruism. My muses have always been gentleness and beauty; my object always to invent wisdoms burst childhoods yet might not doubt. Doubtless the breath energy that pours truth into my verse is the same kindness that flows amongst well-met humanitarians. I guess my entire vocation could be an excuse to dwell here, in this spirit of gorgeous conversation and charity. Volunteers indulge a visceral passion for purposeful work; like good poets, volunteers move hearts. People give their busy selves to further empathy, thankfulness, intellectual freedoms, and human rights; they remind themselves of worthy perspiration. Unusual understandings are gained as pity and apathy's sighs, spent for those who we see as dispossessed, are humbled by the talent caring demands. Caring competently is work; it's listening to the mess, it's waiting for the gut instinct; it's choosing truth over style. The self drops itself in order to give. I want—to give. Feel that in-tension? It's not selfish, it's might brimming over, it's the body understanding our earthly, ecological interdependence at heart level. My usefulness wants to extend itself into many branches. What more important, worthy achievement than thoughtfulness, repeated over and over, in daily devotion? I want to give what I can, this rhyme, as if words could build in vocal materials of sound an unhierarchitecture; as if I might make soft space, structurally, inside bodies, inside practical heads. A place to mentally rest, a worship-ful drumbeat, a centre, radiating. The flow, flow of words, of thought, the flow of interconnection and love could emanate, pump, breathe, from that space of emptied-out ego. A beautiful shit-givers flow, through veins and gesture and arteries and gifts and money; the slow oscillating of relation-ship, laking in the gut-hollow of mindfulness. The body knows the plea-sure of gather and release; of furious accumulation and furious spend; of eat, yes, and excrete. The pleasure of giving is bodies' measure of finely being tuned to all that lives. Our benefit is to give a shit, y'all, because Earth's respiration is in the shit you give.

39

O holy night, what should my words do at this wishful time? Humans want their Charismatic Day. I sing when night thoughts star the dark familiar holiday theatre. A better poet's art softens me when that cynical enmity threatens to make me disown praise. A poet whose mind frees its owned self brings a kindness I wish for, that isn't about making sincerity shows for occasion. When Emily praised, the space between her verbs opened onto formless, ethereal consciousness and let us drift above its depths. Would that Wisława's wise verse animated our dinner conversations, or that her love's eloquence seeped into family get-togethers! If only June's jingles were intoned in the malls! People might buy back their lost selves, by paying visionary attention. Tonight may I give that sweet duende to those sad-hearted, whose gifts reach out hopefully toward undeserving takers. Christmas loneliness mourns the absence of fellowship that wants story and meaning, of kin that would strengthen our practice of love. We gather together to imitate a normal family that hardly exists, but our likenesses find pleasure in comforting avoidance, in taking sweet leave together from commitments. There are those happy families, resembling each other, whose intimacies we either inhabit or have to struggle to achieve. The rest of us love awkwardly, shoving purchases at family members, adding and subtracting from the account of our generosity. These poems delight a sensibility so sweet and acutely seldom cultivated, that despite their craft and expensive inspiration, they do not charm most of the fellow humans I treasure. Couldn't the sonnet be how to make an occasion felt? What if instead of buying, we praised in mad flyting the epic mystery of our togetherness? Brother, for whom I stupidly forgot to purchase a thing, let this evidence of your gift prove your mattering to me.

Terre quakes. La Marseillaise moves quietly along avenues, moves quietly along Boulevard Voltaire, quietly, along Philippe-Auguste, shaken, the Marseillaise walks, holding placards, through a long past that opens out into the present, moves down Rue de Malte, chants, holding up shared ideals, the belief in more knowing, along Avenue Parmentier, quietly, along Chemin Vert, the attentate threat hovering over us, la Marseillaise sings to tyrants a strained true patriot love, calling to rural islamophobias news of Merabet's faith, imagining times before that vowed *Je suis Charlie*, past barricades, past this humourless moment, when editors fight for blasphemy, along La Rive Droite, the song pushes, solemnly along Avenue de la République, the silence grieving, its quiet loading canons, the unspoken to blame for this, la Marseillaise flows unarmed citizenry along Boulevard de Ménilmontant, showering grateful applause on cops, touching sub-machine guns quietly kept below the belt, bare arms around uniformed watchers wisp bisoux for the military selflessness, decorating the quiet avenues with banners, the whimsy of wilful tastelessness pouting for now, hate-inciting speech quietly telling itself refutations, la Marseillaise streams into editorials, forgiving ethical mockery, the profane rabble moved to starry-urgent lyricism, the anthem arousing, deafened, along the Boulevard de Magenta, the critic who uncomfortably listens, all the verses' war-like lyrics, masking worry, the poor versus the fraternity, along Rue de Lagny, then quietly, along Rue du Morvan, the people not knowing if they risk a greater grief by tolerating habits of eastern religion, if a veil is a greater wrong than hate, among claims to know who earns injury, la Marseillaise moves, as civilly as we do, shouldering disgrace, moving with discomforting anti-Algerian ill will, swelling, showing how words can kill meaning, witnessing shameful displays by hypocrites, its bloody poetry muttering that we must not be foes.

Threats of terrorism are interpretable. Their sneaky wrongness, their threat to liberty, is committed by terrorists who are recognizable by monitors. Homeland security is measured by scent. If you are not scheming, then why whine about government watching you? Maybe authority and mouthy yahoos like you can't be friends. You know full well that behaviour infuriates the forces, but you will tempt fate until someone follows you somewhere that you can't report. Guess who won't let a house of Parliament counter-act? Concede, therefore, that you will be watched over, on websites, at institutions, at checkouts, through credit card transactions, in health-care information, in networks, via cable broadcasters' tracking television views and broadband widths, on screens, at work, by implanted browser cookies, with tax software, on cameras. Notwithstanding some unwilling submission, your loyalty will be harvested and checked for terrorist likelihood. We have privatized privacy; it's now more qualified to arrest non-aryan men who but barely demonstrate behaviour. Our mighty security economy sees threat like a frontier to be aggressive about. Canadian children must apprehend scaredy-babies as nauseating, yet understand that morally straying youth are everywhere, foreigners leading them with messaging aimed at their patriotism. Even brothers in underwear, brothers in basements, right now could be under art's forces. We will disrupt behaviour before attacks can even be thought. Words found blinding truth with fear shall be quickly and ruthlessly bent to authority. Attempts to think might endanger reaction, brother, so quiet. Something evil beyond apathy is breaching a vulnerability you believe unbugged. Our defences shall seize terror's media.

Threading culture through Shakespeare, I confront my inheritance, mis-
given. Not all my grief is languaged, yet it may be said: this locution
grieves. I am daughter of tides of war—really, tides of merchant ships,
same thing. The map the British desired continues to fold my wailing into
itself; I have no chief to nation my loss. My fragile genealogy proves that
the powerful teach themselves memory only when memory affirms roy-
alty. My blood's a vintage of offenders and the abused; a line of white cells
sexed with cursed bloody red. My father's people vaunted crosses they held
over heads; my mother's, subjected to Britain's Guyanese system—whether
negro or Hindu, they knelt to Westminster. I love the root of language
and its forms, even if my psyche gacks her nerves' responsive condition-
ing to snobbish English. Amerindian Carib sounds survive in me—tones
nuff nuff be ring in me hed steady na—flickers of intimate contact of
bodies, of origins' etymology, still exist as me, liking a voice that sounds
so. My ancestry will disappear into what's over whenever I finally lose the
memory game. That loss will seal my colonial version's gain, and losing
that version of myself white friends hated shamefacedly will compound
that loss. But through this appropriate voice we find each other, angry and
guilty, oppressed and bossy, the twains that my hindbrain, tongue-tied,
stomachs. For memory's sake I lay aggroculture on memory's thespian
scripture. Goldsmiths brutalize the generative spirit; they jack unprop-
erty; their unmemory frames the digital endless as tone-deafly as Saartjie
Baartman was framed by Doctor Dunlop. Won't it be sweet flattery when
they turn their smart machines on me? Shakespeare will forever subutter
my restated colonial legacy.

When women walk outside, advertisements wink at their underclothes. Magazines draw eyes to airbrushed bustlines, hairless white forearms, liquid liners, leather handbags, lacy thongs. Beauty advice whispers things under respectable ladies' breath, in undertones women hide under foundations. Brazilian waxes and epilation devices remove hair from places that men try to look on, though some men demand that head hair, too, be kept modestly invisible. Righteous North Americans *ban* head coverings. That tuft, muffing vadge, of hair is reckoned undesirable (clipped or trimmed is barely tasteful)—but heads had better not be shorn or tucked under wraps that we associate with shahs. Plucked brows and shadowed lids, lashes done with mascara, make brown or light eyes show womanly, artful, seductive pitch in any shah or president's country. Womanish form for many is just shapely play-show to the clueless male, like those drag-for-a-day white youth, who try Hallowe'en queeny with moustache and muscle, who want an experience of starlight, but who can return to masculinity when seeing eyes threaten to gay-bash. A gender performance, as if cheeky attention-getting is all it is! Womanish power, others would likely say, is mobilized in lined eyes and subtly noticeable breasts; shrewd girls make doors open by looking good. When the definition of worthy feminine accomplishment is inviting dudes' arousal, young women show genius undeliberately, as do young men (who might get it hazed away). But fair ladies who promptly perfect their shapely deportment, or who ignore outfit strategy's hip-hugging imperatives, lose a beauty of sleep wondering if their insights are less visible than their pretty eyes. Looks don't exhaust a girl's strategic energy, necessarily, but looking for kind regard can. Boys may retort that manliness fights to see its wiles realized, that women sell-cheap themselves as armcandy. My nonconforming greenlights brighter days, when advertised ambitions don't fashion these binaried weathers of successful femme.

44

In fibre optic threads, the full insubstantial force of economy's flow pulses. Somewhere, someone thought up an injurious genius: that distance should not stop information or money. Meanwhile a body's form still in three and four dimensions occupies its goblet of space. Oil and wood and automobiles need still be brought from one local microclimate, safely, to another. Remote areas, where essential housing and food costs are astronomical, are yet still informationally (however intermittently) hooked in to all the global buzzing. Offshore money flows almost immediately from debit cards to mutual funds, from outposts in the farthest reaches to your pocket's charge card. Money moves independent of real commodity; digitally held tender flows across nations' embargos as legit cashouts. Light can jump both sea and land: so also does information corporations and militias might wish sneakily deleted. Photos reply-alled accidentally are whisked across the digisphere, showing up in your social media. Bodies are all but anachronistic. They ought to make physicality obsolete—hook us to machines that shit, eat, and mate in our stead; let thought travel global cables into virtual planes, freeing souls from the leaden weight of physical form. Families would hook their infants to the involutionary matrix before their growing synapses are bound too tightly to musculature. So much of earth and water would be restored, if humans gave up physical movement. Impossible, of course. Material reality persists; even digital information needs its cables and resistors; bank vaults now store whopping architectures of money and commodity data, where once they stored cash notes, silver ingots, and gold. The human thought-body extends from flesh to movement of pens and keyboards into forms, letters, and work. Work's body used to be weighed in the heavy metals. Our energy wavers, as labour adapts to surges of electronically etherized resource woe.

They want a voice that performs its wry ownership of literary pedigree, that airily scatters namedrops into a liturgical giving of finger. Matthew Arnold elaborated on the flawless logic that hears genius wherever genius abides: those first-rate men seriously thought, they seriously felt, and their musicality demonstrates their sincerity. Although these days, a straight presentation of bare sentiment isn't white. The same whiteness filter, their discriminatory presumption, slides over full-colour whiteness that doesn't obsequiously back their genealogy. Can I get an amen? Editors at venerable publishing houses want pre-eminentness or wunderkinder, maaaybe Blackness discreetly softened into lyric-not-invective, a vogue like Langston Hughes' or Zadie Smith's. How gracefully Claudia confided her being mad! someone effused to juries. I'd write cheeky kowtows to literary lions and university insiders in skylark-happy strains, adding touches of knowingness—not of prejudice's affects, but of the oppressor's burden —to witty, blithe metaconfessionals, if the absence of what's outlawed, my unliterary shrill, didn't fuel this composition. I blurt embarrassing, inappropriate speech. Curators, annoyed by the nervousness my twitch inflicts on company, make notes to selves not to get L'Abbé for shows; where's that suretongued frontman Snicket? These workshops aren't for venting abuse; they're not therapy! bellow instructors—men who back up against the asses of young protégées, declaring softcore fresh and gritty. To be fair, when I was idealistic and thought race could be uninvented through winning, I insisted on my sameness. I thought if I just could write the joyless blockbuster of truth, explaining once and for all wrongheaded privilege's unreliable lead, I'd get kissed by blond, athletic former bullies gobsmacked by my phrasing. There, I've done it again. Disqualified my brand. No sonnet market expands—whining haters, grudging fellows, understand.

My intermittent employment and my hard-earned microstardom deny
each other. Am I not important? Am I not stalwart? How to admit the
university is dead? That the conquest of arts' humanity is downright? My
qualifications once meant employment—now my heart's thirst compares
its dismay with pink-slipped manufacturing workers. Hindsight would
berate me for following my heart when any imaginative eye ought to have
foreseen the doom of further education. However, the weight my heart
would hoist, if helplessly it had had to withdraw from the circular path
of actualization! Humanities may die on institutional principle, but the
articulation of dreams and honest oath will never be priced. The body
records with accuracy what institutional eyes don't buy; the unauthorized
story needs its defenders—humanities do the truths that people circum-
stantially deny. Industrial demands are why citizens invented human-
ism; the more industry profanes its creative people, all the more human
resourcefulness is enslaved to survival mode. But in what meetspace, if not
in universities, will digital culture's disciples demand patience in the telling
of education's quest? Who forms thoughts, if all thoughts are turned to
wants the corporate machine totally hearts? Maybe not dubious university
theorists, whose rare versions and dictions condescend to the very story-
minded hearts that seek clear-eyed vision. But most university humanists
defend the dear heart's part. Advocates for the just, not just the bottom
lines, they see their status erode and budgets diminish as the youth war
on underemployment. I still mean to work at art. And though this market
breaks my heart, I sell human right to metaphysical accounts. My reward's
a class of poverty and fortune financial charters cannot chart.

Between dioxins in fatty meats, warnings about genetically modified organisms, random sulphates in baking powder, vegetables tasting of produce-antimicrobials, tomato alkaloids' poisoned reputation, cheeses' deadly proteins, BHA, good fats, sugar's insulin blow-ups, lactose intolerance, rBST, rBGH, bean sprouts' hospitality to bacteria, white bread equalling death, and toxic vitamin regimes, my system is famished for real food knowledge. Over the teeth and through intestines, look out, liver, it's not just wines that strain through reddish hilum. Morsels of food touch the smooth interior of swallowing throat, slimy all over, spit-mucin tongued, already its starch broken down by amylase, through pharynx, down through food pipe via peristalsis, past glands' secretion, through the sphincter and into expandable stomach. Banquet binges extend stomachs' stretchy shape—that torte, that noodle, that butter chicken roti, meet mucosa and protein-breaking enzymes inside my chyme maker, then they are intestinal guests. There pancreatic digestives and yellowish bile swish with organic juices in gut hollows. Stuff is absorbed. Gut flora make vitamins and prevent bad bugs' growth. An ecosystem shares that part of us; we host dinner parties for thousands of bacterial microbes with every mouthful. Yeasts and probiotic lactose-munching fermenter organisms make fatty acids that lower ventral pH; that acidity squelches farts. The way of the gastric tract demands presence, a sitting still with meals, for though we know exactly how breakfast turns into us, the power of tasty chemicals and yummy starches hooks our highest minds on cravings. My diet moves along inside me, from mastications' moist first principles to long-winded, bitingly heated exchanges; ruminations end either as lady weight or utter shit. The swallowed conversation of plant and flesh, the earthly soil redecomposing itself, the daily practice of nutritiously reconstituting my ass is both gross and outta sight! Aww is at work when the small baby researches materiality by putting thingamabobs in her mouth. Naïvely she trusts taste and smell to embody her cells' delight.

48

How careful must walkers be, if Black when walking. Too freaking many Black walkers are history. Not for treacheries, but trifles, are men under terrorful arrest's bars too often thrust. The atmosphere of terror, for many, results less from international militias' fighting words or unsuspected domestic betrayers, and more from those command-followers, police, who foster falsehood, instead of understanding they are wards of trust. Bullying sergeants' authority comes out of laws that once named some men property. Ask Jimmie Crow which people understand how race influences target-embodiment, how states with low morale create antipathy and comfort landowners by naming an enemy. Americans' greatest grief wants to buy a house, obey stop signs, find a life partner. The worst American diminishment only cares to signal before turning left; to be the potential prey of one slavery-mouthed, vulgar, trigger-happy officer's enforcement; to achieve greatness or have it thrust upon him; to not get locked up in any charlatan investments; to leave well enough alone. Race is a thought the Americas' plantations cotton-mouthed; a vicious negging that is felt as repellent. If you aren't recognized within the gentlemen's enclosure of supremacy, brother, arrests for random whatever are at their convenience. Only at their pleasure, breather, you may respectfully come, say sir, and maybe disappear. Trayvon, Dante, Victor, Walter, Tony, Tamir, Michael, and Eric, you're on a list of "shot unarmed" on Gawker; I looked you up. Today a badge was let off for killing Rekia. What fear your form of truth proves. "Feeling threatened" is evidence video won't show. Fuk da police, said Dre, *sa prize!*—his smile could be so disarming.

49

Whoa, Tanya Tagaq's   instants iighm. Tanya Tagaq   ughm, breathes as i   o e e   e atone time come.   i E i , epiglottal linguish she eethees   o   hhwn,   ghnm,   e hwygh under affects. When a hsthy vocal she heaves, her breath a e i o i u   o   suhmn. a a   e to that auditory body; cardiovascular i   u : respect's a gutteral i i . at yghma i e come when   ou hmsha allaha at strangled lyric, past strangled scarce. Screely   ee   e,   i   hwth and throatsung oa , with ungh energy hewshed i o o , o e e   o the strict Brit thing i a . Ahoosh aha,   eau i u A   e a ea e amid sons' professionalized ghhrgg. O settler langwedges' extractive logic, Tanya Tagaq uighnhs u e a e   e ii a e   u e. Oi   orchestral, au i i symphonic, the vein system ea   e e, with inbreathed   o   e e of mining, outbreathed o   e   e of tundra, self-preservation and chthonic u i ion. y flesh a e e , a e e , brainstemmed y self uproars earthroat cunnilingual unword. y e a u   industreal in songs' tonalpathy, punk Arctic. To sound like a wolverine, like a porpoise, thrum in the throat, i a u ii . A sound i o e coo, e- u strength of polar a u , i u i a a i , ie whale cry in tonal convulsation with electronics. To me, Tagaq's a i aa ululates and ungnhs the regenesis of au e.

50

L

How heavy would the self-possession journey be, if on the way no other women published their own hunts for what I seek. My weary travel is lightened by dark accounts that teach me that the ease I want, that nod, that respect and composure, are not-impossible in a day-to-day that thus far hasn't relinquished the material desirables of race. Distance is measured outward from wealthy friends' kitchen tables. You can sit at that table if you arrest memory. I am tired with my woe, but so are you; history's consequence plods dully on. Poetry is born to bear that weight, to intone the measure of self-inflicted blame, and yet hear some perfect instinct of the wretched vindicated. We know history's understoried verses and true loves; we do not speechify; we endure being made from the impulse beneath the bloody spur. I cannot provoke history's monsters; they swat at my bothersome, timeless anger as cattle unthinkingly brush at bees; the giant oafs of history lurch ideologically toward whiteness and new chauvinisms. When heavily my heart answers these teeny microslights with a groan, their pique more sharp to me than spat slurs, then do your writings rally to this human's side. For the soul-mate sameness of your groan doth produce quiet empathies in my mind; my grief's loneliest hour finds inward company, and my joy of scribbling approaches its kind.

The hustler can make money. She loves how cash excuses the spender's lowest offences. Official money dulls bull-detectors best; treasurers' white collars confuse prosecutors aiming for thieves. Being respectable deflects all sorts of comment. White collars bet on housing markets, watch Bay Street exchange stock, pull down six figures, chase debtors, embolden stakeholders' confidence, fill tills, improve returns, offer positions to eager juniors. No need for white collars to make excuses for white collar gimme; how many poor beasts suit themselves in fine duds, whipped in swish outfit? The extreme city changes faces unremittingly. But slowly the upmanship of the hustler, the dispassionate hustler, throws its pugilistic bohemia around. The downtown heavies want in. Doing winged speed in promotion's bathroom stalls, politicking, our whiteshirted friend can ball. No workhorse can with money's desire keep pace, therefore debts are incurred, therefore fortune's perfect stooges labour while the clever's fortunes are being made. It is hallowed as moneychangers in God's house, as kingdoms of God full of camels that greased their entrée through innocent needles' eyes, the fainthearted rally against the rat race. But love, you say, for love the hustler surely has a small trust? Excuse my jaded song—since the fall I sing from the ego's calculating, not the downtrodden heart. I will not fraudulently sing of love when the owed are dunces; the true creditors fail to collect. Hustlers run the Canada I know; give me the inside mark, or else where can value's vector go?

Some dreamers idealise the rich, whose blessings plainly hoodwink equity. The canny bride's ring exhibits her smart method: his sweet setup locked down her treasure, and there is a witchiness to her charm he will not ever query. The flavour of sugar in every performance. Despite a blunt rationing of authenticities, their finely appointed confederation seldom lacks pleasure. Their efforts inspire dreamers' efforts. Idealists, so solemn and so rarely satisfied, decry affluence, but seldom compel quite even themselves to give up striving. Trenchantly we long to be the unyearning set. We like stories of good business, of worthy fortune hunters who play fair and do things openly, whose place among the privileged is earned. If our captains and their jewelled significant others care, we can keep our dignity while swabbing their ebony-inlaid decks. The material game that keeps you at your desk, the money headaches that thorn a desire to change one's wardrobe to one which less matches your obedience, are the conditions in which ideas, transformative lakes of mental speculation, petal into substantiality. The specially blessed get to body the new unfoldings of *ch'i*'s simple creation, to succeed beyond sex's prides and joys. But lesser dreamers, are they, who just want a nice house? Who roll with inequities and misgivings? Realistic dreamers cope with being human. Idols extol triumph, being idols. Who, the archetypal knucklers down? Who teach us how to be the one percent?

What idiot says out loud they're on substance at work? Here is the office, the space where ballyhoo is suitably made; here is the voice that moves millions. Of the strange things done in shadows no one savvy speaks aloud! Confessional tercets aren't very on trend—have they ever been, really? Only the lonely throw shade at the hand that feeds. You are but one comrade in the very shadowy play of ends met; describe no addictions, insanities, or deathwishes that could interfere with responsibilities. The poor royalty imitate a shocked affectedness for you on the television during psych health week: they're all, "flaws are part of beauty" on-set, and off, shun you. In Grecian times, oracle professionals breathed pythia and intranced new speaking, but offices would rather an inspiring manager defame, as poison, unofficial traditional healing. You're earnest, that's less commendable than our videos attest. The shadows of your beauty should never whisper the other aspects of your body-mind's untidy domesticity; the rule of appearance should command you in every blessed shape. We don't need to know anything past loyal, external graces. In your personal life candour might have some part, but you'll be liked by no one, and no one will save you, if your cunning can't constrain your heart-to-heart.

Our mother owes much more dough than she breadwins. Dutifully she
has breadwon for us, toiled for us. We see Mom buy that sweater or that
garden tool and our dependent temperaments twitch—do rich kids trust
what doting mothers give? Our mother owes the balance between the
books and a fair shake, but fair-minded lenders won't forgive the disinter-
est she dares embody. For that sweater or mentholated rub is our citizen-
ship, which doesn't come cheap. In the Whig heart we lived as the canker
blossoms that serve the graft of cultural ascendance, the paid yes-wallah's
ineluctable children, performing an unmentionable, undetermined cul-
tural nonpresence. Our father rose at four-thirty, a shame hanging over
his unassuming citizenship, the forward motion of his work and play dis-
sipated in slavewagery. A generation of poorly whelped consumers: my
mother's sobriety fathered what my father's icefrogged manhood—not his
skin—defied. Best buds disclose tips, but my father was a forced togeth-
erer, his distressed virtue only wishing not to have to make a mug's insin-
cere show of togetherness. My body lived unwooed and unrespected, but
my fabulous, educated mind might be suited to themselves, Whigs saw.
That sweater and that expectorant performed my mother's wishes, then.
I don't owe the sums my mother does; my father's retired into his sweater
and anesthetic; the deal my mother signed earned us our own sweaters and
apartments. Today our self-made parents' debt is the despot of our scrappy
house. We, the beauteous and lovely youth, know when the sweater shop
finally fails, our grind-employed and overdrawn servant leaders will still
synonymize our truth.

Priscila, you're not made of impenetrable defences, thank God. You're the gifted social doer, dreaming monumental achievements, holding friends close. Anti-princess, you shall outlive this; you are the powerful rhymer, bringing about your visions. You shall shine more brightly in thirty years, gracing more tables of contents than umpteen sweating competitors, mentoring more young urban scribes, with more swagger in your old woman's little finger, than bookslut hotties half your age. With wry intimacies between the known and mysterious are your beautiful words starred! You shall be statuesque in the over-seventy fun runs, embarrassing dudebro senior athletes daring to set foot in your tracks. The work of your dream masonry will build new normals for those who shelter in books and honest words. Your written word, warm with your vision's quick fire, symphonically burns the living record of your memory into the page, and ingrains that enduring expectation of life, of being here in life's grandness, into us all. You're a badass livestream, glorious enemy of self-pity and shallow efforts. You set the pace for self-styled superachievers; your praise puts blush on a baller's cheek; you'll still be finessing grand ballrooms when you're ninety-seven. You're already immortal in the eyes of all writerly posterity. Tell death to wait, you're busy karaokeing, wearing this world out until the very end, wringing every drop of remarkableness from this blink of woke. All the joy, understanding, and bedazzlement that shine from your self-awareness becomes our lives' weather, as you live in this world and radiate wellness into a zillion more novels, parties, poetry books, and friends' hearts.

Sweet talker, your voice renews my faith in delivery. You never force or bludgeon with opinion. Who is it that said your pitch's sly edge should be as blunt as butter? Maybe theirs was an appetite for something which butter couldn't satisfy, but which by feeding on attention was temporarily allayed. Politico, motivator, I am roused by your wit, your sharp repartee; I am weakened in the proverbial knees. My former self might say, *so this is love,* this objectifying hold of your focus, enthralling my thoughts of democracy and coding thoughts of evilly slandering other objects of your hungry eyes. I can't even with the silly teehees your wink wrings from my faithful girliness. Tomorrow I'll see you again and do my best not to kill the spirit of responsible government within which we act out this perpetration, this mutual fraudulence simulating respect. Let me treat this draw like a shady internship, a mutual frisking, where we test the oceanic possibilities of depth while our commitment-phobic, political hearts stay on the shore. Where two shrewd, contractually restrained networkers come daily together, banging out hooks, an attractive work chemistry is bound to seethe. Your communication strategies rely on turn of phrase—I love you, more, as subtle satire. Maybe I take the ironic view, or call it what it is: banter, which, being the faultless language of the careless, makes a poet's fundamentals tremble. Your style wields such likeness of care, for me, ethnographer of sincerities more wished for and more rare.

Offline, I still believe in reading, in poetry, in slow culture. On social media, am I visible? What should I do but aim to trend? I use an app to manage the hours of absentminded time I spend scrolling fruitlessly down curated desires, but I have no sense of precious time at all once my attention locks into the opendlessness of streaming services. The story doesn't end; a serial-like storyness is our new questish narrative. In antistory, how do I dare? Millennial children know the world-without-end as hoax; the future whiles away, as governments bargain money and sovereignty against water's cleanliness. The atmospheric clock lurches forward and only stories without conclusion pretend a soothing. The kinesthetic, birthed tenderness of reading bodies tries patience: as our wishes unyoke our heads' aggressive ambition from the body's hour-servant condition, we bid the creaturely adieu. I want to read a realizing, the antiquest, a post-conclusion, wrighting in cursive hand my jealous thoughts and wishes (censored from my online automatism) into an energy, an embodiment, of the storyteller's punctuation. The caesurae of my feed, those unassuming bars of #d8dfea between squares of people's posts, imperceptibly iron out the lived kinesis, the abrasive and gesticulative beats that say beast, glandular, earthling. Like a chute of never-enough, the smart devices' downrush of personalized clickworthy is our appetite's groove, a hangry flow channel. People. There is a y and another y in this procedure. I make these poems from text's ulterior matter. Upstream, if you have followed this line woven through bardic tapestries, denotify your network. Your will endures through your reading. You make the unstory of this english sonneteer, this kink, snagging loops in the scrolls of influence.

Let that shit go, forebrain. Dismiss the atrocity meandering still in memory. To first traumas you remain slave, if the shadows of ugly doings stalk your thoughts and control your times of pleasure. Cortex, be rational! Psychological understanding should mean deleting the neural account of terror's hours. Terror, cranium? You overdo it, habit, exaggerating your juvenile assaults, boohooing when understatement would more strategically disclose your snivel. Nerves, write an erasure over the latent shame that suffers beneath this bitching, boombastic lyric! Hormones, bury my boogie men in nice enkephalins! You said that already. You are imprisoned in a brain's sentence, which conforms to your limbic lobe's circuitry, and try the patience of mainstream poets, who suffer no redundant utterance. So my brain deliberates, running cliché checks on its own image storehouse, my psyche accusing my psyche of cuckooing from injury. Be where you are, lamas insist, so I type out raw characters, from impulses so strong that only my corpus collosum, that anonymous author, knows itself, phenomenally . . . ah. What privilege to age this way, working out this era's terrorisms' affects on a wholehearted body, outwitting psychological torture-play, documenting a stamina some documents wish blotted—the long memory of our self-hatred and the will to pardon, if the offence, the self-undoing crime of humiliation, were metabolized in the awareness of the nation. Though awareness of our humiliating aggression is a sober hell, denial and other-blame systematizes our pleasure, and becomes our architecture, until neural conciliations recode us well.

Don't sniff at aromatherapies! Rose oil may be nothing new, but its therapeutic witcheries are big biochemistry. Turkish attars and herbal medicines hand-laboured from roses know how aromantic, how meek, our brains are when beguiled by whiffs of biochemical ambrosias. Luring olfactorily is English lavender's vocation: we buzz like charmed bees at mint's cousins' purple breath. The scent of conifers, of cedar burned, of the pines of a northern forest, of mountain juniper, may be merchandised as golden disinfectants but also speak the ancestral record of Cherokee smoulderings. Witch hazel bark calls oo-e- a- e- a- e to red-looking skin. Even forty-five, fifty-five hundred courses of the sun still haven't unknown its name. I like mossy odours, despite aroma sages' insistence on mosses' masculine mystique: I smell like a boy, like an oak smelling the branched mind of plant fibres. My sweet jasmine character was dominated by the plantation's manuring—hatreds tended toward hatreds—so the sweet absolute was crushed. The woman, the girl, in me decomposes in a musk of ladies' homey apathy. The oil of this decomposition smells of sandalwood, coriander, and tobacco flower; of hyssop, curry leaf, oregano, and myrtle. What fireweed, i a a a or `æ ə , or a e u u , knows is grounded in scorched whereabouts; its sweet stem, its root-healing syrup and odour whisper the crushed's revolutionary biology. Ethereally this amuse-nez atomizes erasure's incense amidst the writings of former days, to air out subjects that other words (bouquets) have cognitively musked in self-administering praise.

60

Local IKEAs outfit houses with alsvik faucets, smaka cheese cutters, botne wardrobes, spathiphyllum potted plants, klubbo coffee tables, lindsdal handles and knobs, norreskog odorous candles, format cabinet lights, nutid exhaust hoods, and kajsa sten duvet covers. Their blue and yellow architectures are harbingers of indistinguishable places with stylish coordinates, with irreproachably organized closets. Before IKEA's consequential interior imperialism, loveseats were forever. Now temporary is how decorators do contemporary condo. Somnat cribs, svit cutlery, koncis steel roasting pans, fantast meat thermometers, aina cushions, fläckig white colanders and bowls, tomat spray bottles, titta djur finger puppets, groggy corkscrews and heat trivets go with betydlig and hugad curtain rods, alve drawer units, fredde computer workstations, kritter children's chairs, liatorp bookcases and glass cabinets, and thorine polyester hedgehog pillows. We're years post–*Fight Club* and still they send me the catalogue, that seductive document, that porn of Swedish furnishings; my gift card props the INGKA Foundation up; their glossy merch doth me transfix. The careful layout of retail showrooms is contrived to convey you through a long, winding, deliberate groove, counterclockwise, past shelves and partitions, along slow aisles of cheap Scandinavian beauty, past bins and rows of textiles and fashion kitchenware. The sardonic market for medium-density fibreboard must be one of nature's truths; what would stand in clothing stands' thereabouts if not for this basic home accessory itch? When customizing your window treatment, don't you dwell on cost like any customer? I've spent more time on this than I meant to. I should put this item away. I never had a taste for Swedish meatballs until I needed a nightstand; but o! disproportionate injustice! when—godlike—they wouldn't rethink, despite my girlish dissent, the cruel height limit of småland.

I sit at the screen, hoping you will facetime. Should I delete your image? Should I keep tabs open? Maybe you're a douche avoiding any reply to my emails, but you said sometimes you're just prohibitively weary. Like this nightie? Does it fetch your desire? I'm very close to deleting your number, asshole, but ladies like me will be your bootlicker if you're nice. Why not even a smiley face? You're shady, I know it. I must like to suffer these degradations. Are you mocking my selfies? Ghosting me? Is it apathy, or your spirituality, that thwarts your ability to hit send? Shelter from the suffering is all I hope for, and you're from my hometown. I noticed on your myspace that your drummer bailed. It's not totally prying to find out your shows and games and idle bullshit on a public platform, is it? Answer me. Together, lovers cope and navigate an unsure world! My faith, not my jealousy, is what's owed acknowledgement here; you got *love*, even though your music, honey, is not so great. It is my love that keeps me interested even though your likeability wanes. I keep a mental inventory of moments when true love broke through your attitude, and know that fundamentally you are sweet—it just doesn't show often. A little companionship is all I ask. Lately the watchman, or whatever the name is for the guy who sits at the desk in the foyer downstairs, has been watching me. While you chill somewhere with the phone turned off, why don't I just walk—to somewhere else, wherever the foyer guy's the romantic lead, and I'm the fair, long-suffering heroine, whose life is about to change forever, but she suffers just a little bit more before living happily ever after.

Your residential schools fostered lifelong survival modes. Dispossessing Tsleil-Waututh, Malahat, Qualicum, Plains Cree, Îyâhé Nakoda, Hesquiaht, Onondaga, Yellowknives, Passamaquoddy, Stó:lō, Innu, Blackfoot, and Algonquin children of family took effort. Government money paid for cruelty and for this sin there is no remediation yet. This act is so grounded in white supremacism, so backward thinking, that my heart spasms, rethinking professionalism. The "true north" face of settler goodness-gracious is so polite. Assumption, Alberni, Cross Lake, Breynat Hall, Cape Dorset Hostel, Résidence Couture, Wawanosh Home: out the truth of such accounts, administered formally by Ryerson and Campbell Scott. Fort Vermilion, Lestock, Crowstand, Wawanosh, Crowfoot, Shubenacadie, Bishop Horden, Battleford Industrial, Federal Hostel at Frobisher Bay, File Hills, Norway House: out the administration of all that work, the professionalism, the murder-mouthing, the responsible educators. When "my" country's gentlemanliness shows me myself, I'm West Indian; when "my" education does, I'm subaltern. At the Cobourg Foodland I'm chopped liver with tanned skin, but I am never called Iroquoian. This country, said mine, says an ownership my self-love quietly resists, turning contrarily to the i ê i a o i of Turtle Island. Self-consciously I research schoolfellowed languages to verbalize the thing white privilege, by definition, isn't. Three equity committees this week asked for my counsel, for that informant-befriendly-pleasing I want to believe effects something. Praise Jesus, proclaimed the Dene elders invited to the policy thing, when "like, a ceremony or a smudge?" was what my director wanted. His embarrassment was reputational. Body of Christ, they had me say. I say it to you, Chief Justice.

Agricultural instinct means the Jersey's lowing moves no hands to stall the butcher's meat supply. Dairy farmers know cows. A bovine mother's time is meted in jugs; her periods and estrous cycle are the cattle managers' headache. How can rushed and overworked women moan when Holsteins' udders have been drained by machines, their metestral blood analyzed, their heads filled with promises of good breeding? How can old wives—who, despite their lines and wrinkles, who, despite long ago having passed youthful mountability, remain husbanded, thwarting procreative natural laws—denounce the mechanized production age? Even some ants know to keep honeydew-anused aphids wingclipped and herded. The animals do agricultural things: who says we are no better than hunters if we consume cow flesh? My vegan friend scoffs at anyone who eats meat or drinks anything dairy, but every now and again she ingests cheese, forgives herself a nice salmon quiche. She doesn't understand why more folks don't fight the system that milks; she's also a lesbian programmer who gets barfy at the mention of pregnancies, nursing, amniotic fluid, thick discharges, antepartum hemorrhaging. Foremen eat such atrocities for breakfast. Farmers don't entertain the cow's discomfort: if they can't get an instrument comfortably inside far enough, they'll find another instrument. Language is the cruel knife that cuts human umbilicalness forever, cutting from memory mommy's wetbreasted lovetaste from boys' ejaculatory thoroughbreeding. Sodomy *loves* horses; we like to forget. Between the city and the supermarket is the Bible, cautioning country bucks to husband but clean animals, reminding the breeders not to mate siblings. Girls act like fillies, like nice workhorses, hoping to be seen and bought. Their milky breasts have full lives underneath. Meanwhile, ladies in shopping centres find their pumping in public still aggravates leathery men.

When I have, as usual, been the banal only-minority-in-the-room, my face hasn't fallen. Usually I'm thinking about something immediate—a decision. I face down the demographics by habit. I'm proud and the social cost of outing white group segregation is brutal; I'm permitted in *because* I don't interrogate white dominance. There's something we've met to accomplish, but it's not fighting, or querying, the power—it's exercising it. We're in a board room, we're in a restaurant—some zone of coded amnesia—who would be so crass as to make the group uncomfortable? No one's a slave in this room. Onward, with professional demeanour, go we. When I have impulsively been the humourless, angry social justice avenger, I had no friends, and so no advantage among the kingdom's executive officers, in the show of friendship that is Canada. Now the firm soil of winners is below my feet. The water quality here is magnificent. Ignoring colour eases things; we can get on unhindered with development projects, sales and losses, with legislation and rebranding. When I have spoken evenly about such experiences, as if to foster a change of state, a molecular state shift, it is myself I reconfigure. Grounded in the body that faces surfaces, I play the instrument of feeling. The brown hand I was dealt has taught me to hustle and to ruminate but I hate distinguishing myself from white people; if I'm welcome in a green room shouldn't that take my loner vibe away? These tiresome thoughts arise a thousand times a day, uneasy truths which I cannot choose but to wipe from my eyes. So I stop noticing thoughts. I have them, but they float like white characters amidst a fluorescent aura, asking what I've got to lose.

Since those boys rode my ass, I've had no self-respect. The tone of unforgettable underneath my skin. For boys understood that the less self I had, the better to fuck with sad me. Corporeal, they animalled my enmity. Like a dog eager to please, I was. Boys tested their power. How with this rage was I charged with a deflowered, slavish beautyhole; I entered a plea that became my whole body. Some strange action, invisible and no stronger than that flower, must now be through me in words rehallowing this bummer. Else why am I so confessy? I breathe. I'm not holding on to it. My butt, saggier now than in that last collection, but still the wearer of pants and backer of impulses in this relationship, is on the edge of my seat. Okay. The battering media saying squats, weight lifting, gluten-free paleo cooking, fitspiration, impressed me with signs of what's doable. After the operation, I had finally lost, so something gave out, but some interior flood gates of steely resolve stayed strong. My butt, the impressionable child exclaims. The booty apparatus got fearfucked, girl, meditate on that shit! No. We're here now, allowing the backstory but channelling a strengthening methodicalness. I began with stretching, just believing in, well—from there I moved into poses, child's pose always there to curl into and feel hidden, but I was more interested in what shapes strong hands and mind can hold. The isometric exercise makes my weight feel wristed, footed, backed. My core—it withstood their boysport. I might be my own spoiler, goofing up the bad ending their authorship enjoyed. Can your fuck-you do forty burpee-deadlifts? Ronda Rousey is my new crush, the mean girl-armed sensei like whom this bantamweight race challenger might behave. I might still lift the heavy weight borne in Black identifuckyou. My pubococcygeal explosiveness may still push off that intergenerational, abortive fight.

If Titania realized what rascality her husband, jealous, plotted, she'd have set her fairies—Cobweb, Master Mustardseed, Peaseblossom, and Moth—to safeguard her changeling. If Desdemona had kept her handkerchief closer, maybe Iago's treacherous betrayal of Othello would have destroyed fewer. I am but a beggar born, and not the lovely Lady, Tennyson wrote, echoing this rime. The nursemaid in jollity related young, diapered Juliet's first tumbles; Juliet's faith ended unhappily. Men forswore England's king Henry VI and followed Margaret's command; she'd soon be locked up by Edward's Christian men. Flower-de-luces glinted bravely from Joan's vision-propelled blade; she focused a keen-edged maiden's virtue to rescue the dukes of Orléans. Wrongly strumpet-charged was Hermione, jailed and required to give birth to Perdita while fettered. Cordelia's conscientiousness Lear wrongfully disowned, and to Goneril's acquisitive demonstrations, demonstrations Regan exaggerated, he bequeathed territory. No limping sway disabled Katherine, declared Petruchio. Marcus discovered Lavinia, tongueless and mutilated by Tamora's brutish sons; she wrote her rapists' identity in sand. "Folly, doctor-like, controlling skill," Bertrand Russell implied, led to tribunals' monstrous punishments of conscientious objectors. A guilty Lady sleepwalking cried, "Out, damned spot!" while a physician and a trustworthy gentlewoman watched, captivated; hallucinating blood, she orchestrated her own end before her king was decapitated. In fair Ophelia's lap Hamlet laid his brooding head; with pansies, fennel, and columbines the dishevelled, frocked maiden then strew the ground. The Lord's quillibrium begat a sonnet. Shakespeare's verse was throated, this synchronicity embodied. I leave my love along this line.

67

Argh. Where before I wrote this poetry thinking of offences past, I just now a new dishonour lived. He lied, conceivably, when agreeing to boundaries. With his presence I had grown cautiously comfortable; I took his impropriety for courtship. I can't, still, understand how by him such advantage was taken—he took. Fucking hell. What did he achieve, disregarding my delineated no-space? Did he think only of himself? Why give this piece of shit your verse, Sonnet. Because: the anxiety I've written here already was historical trauma, the lived fallout of sexual perpetrations I tried to integrate into my political activism; now everything has changed. Bleck. But changed so unexpectedly—suddenly I'm declarative, suddenly those old emotions got fresh insight. I'm living the culmination of me, always. Why should I pour any more of my beauty into describing the effects of insensibility? Why seek restoration if the losses are absolute? Freshly assaulted, my new power, the resilience that I discovered in poem sixty-five (like, last Saturday), suddenly wrestles a heavy should-have. Like, I should have known from past encounters the bankruptcy of his obsequious fawning; I took his regard for my own fabulous worth. He read these poems—I blush to share such editorial judgment—but his lordliness never really gave in to the soft force of she behind the articulate mesh. None of his exclamations of enlightenment quite honoured the knowledge of abuse that informs my anapests. God, I am proud of my awakeness, it stays alive amidst pressures to prostrate beneath disguised aggressions, but O! haven't I marshalled this poetic, core sensitivity far enough, survived enough? I mean, now what? What new lesson am I to learn through this bullshit exchange? My decisions don't mean diddly? Stop longing for something consensual and sober? Before this little "slip"—little slap to the soul—I thought we had something so bad-ass.

68

Stupid truth. I must quit bullshitting myself. I cheat the workweek, fake the committed application of my days to productive work—I don't know why I circumvent beginning; almost automatically I balk; I have days and days until the deadline and suffer slowly—some errand, some random invitation always consuming me before the sober banalities of task—roundabouting, stressing, mentally scolding myself, suffering accusations from the better worker I mean to be—Procrastinating is an ordeal, an untrustworthiness of habit, grovelling for a living—My brow begging, furrowed, I promise, this time, golden stretches of discipline, I will sow faithfully, blessed expanses of would-be—The spectre of foresight hovers, foreseeing applause, lynchings, boredom I caused, hollow praise, respect—How is respect even fathomable when I'm so nauseatingly beta? Even now my lines are avoidance, another second syllabified, another second phenomenalized in verse when syllabi remain unwritten—Everyone else does what needs flogging; while I sleep away decades, time advances another eager beaver. Somebody else has it in him to choose methodical essay over le fantastique—the hours daydreamed at screens, twittering hours, I let them all go rotten, and mentally acquit myself, and spiritually perjure myself, making the obnoxious excuses all bums mutter, contemptuous of another's greed-driven mojo. I'm robbing someone, or something (a self I don't know, a lost address) and flushing the spoils before my inner authority can retrieve what's undone—is this poem a justification, or a map, or do I pitch a new quality of manure? Let's just recognize that rapey buddy got close by showering you with false admiration. You wanted, sweetheart, to believe he saw authority in the small works you asked of yourself.

LXIX
(for Mila)

The toddler's private parts are so funny. The penises that fathers worry will disturb kids' eyes don't shrink from view. Wankers start in utero, their thingamabobs in their fetal fists, the thought of hooters already taking shape in innocent amniotic dreams. Bums are be-all and end-all; tongues are there to voice explosive fart sounds; lips too give wet, cheeky, blathery farts. Doodlebugs love uttering bare truths, even more so if adult discomfort animates the commentary. Dress-lifters' flashy, outward flirt achieves fullest twirl at formal shindigs; showing underthings is its own reward. With praise caregivers crown the heads of subdued exhibitionists, whose urges to amaze their controlled grown-ups with the sensuality of their genitalia give protective-hearted elders strokes. The innocence of newborn innocence is about everything, fingers and coochies and toes, dodos and bathtime and spit's stringy amazingness, edges and corners and surfaces, out and in. The baby learns peeing feels warm and wet, she learns the diapering rhythms, *wee*, says the hooha, *waa* says the mouth; a soul reaches from within, through holes, to sky. Look at my thing, the toddler thrills; really, behold *me*, ambulatory, orificed, thingly, a mind! Am I not godly and touching? We react; the little ones guess; they measure our bodily, tonal honesty—Dad's voice goes up decibels; Mother turns and coughs. Our hang-ups adulterise their thoughts, although their eyes and willies will, eventually, freak out any inhibitive don'ts we impose. The baby wants fresh air, takes off her clothes, *whoopie!* –her vagina –her *djadja!*—is the centre of her prankish, mischievous delight. Her whole body follows feeling's lead, a starburst where symmetry touches symmetry. *Body!* Our maternal watchfulness fathoms children's somatic authenticity, its bawdy show. Soon the social will instill its prohibitions, and the chasm between their souls and bodies—that xxx, that common cleavage—will grow.

The boats' freight is human. Countries trade rhetoric and blame: the uninvited shall not be our bother; already we accommodate far more castaways than fair economy requires; they land on our borders with no market workabilities; every one we let in just pushes more families to risk their sons and daughters on shady Mediterranean navigations. From Libya, Eritrea, Sudan, Palestine, and Syria, families who suspect traffickers will stow them safely take a flyer on fishing vessels strained with extra voyagers. Oh, Canada—its sweetest air, its forests, hospitals, and crude bitumen are the goods landed immigrants land to get. Nothing but approval impedes their way, their worth to the greater good of Canada being less worry than their colour. We adopt fictions of welcome, of open-armed Canadian kindness, that serve our nice reputation. Why don't *we* answer the moral test posed in Belarus by Donbas deportees? Ha ha, laugh conservatives and other precariously employed resentfuls. That story of a pure, unstained paternalism is so seventies. Meanwhile thousands, hundreds of thousands, of "migrants" have passed by the unblameable cruise ships, government ferries, and uneasy tourists onto unguarded beaches. At Kalymnos, Chios, and Lesbos, the wornout travellers who sailed from Turkey arrive in yachts of rubber, touching beach sand in relief. That jpg of Laith Majid crying— Etter's insta-historic photography—captured an anguish this poem cannot, but even newsworthy pictures can't convince unsympathetic nationals to give up defensive outcry. Every day more people arrive; perimeters are enlarged; if someone has a solution, let's implement it! But the court of ill-masked xenophobia deliberates lethargically. Who will show us the sentiment of The New Colossus now, in a globalized economy, when old kingdoms implode . . . and descendants of huddled masses resist any solidarity show with new huddled masses, who have nowhere to go?

Or can a photo of a lone, lying toddler make mourners of us all? Are we informed now, somehow better than we were in that last poem? Dead child on the sand. Today Europe is "shocked" by the graphic still. From what pleasant concern were they disturbed by this little boy's sullen, cherubic quiet? The senselessness travels, gives warning to the world that Galip and Aylan are no more. They fled not from this vile world but toward it, having applied for asylum to our wonderful home, asking to dwell with us in peace, applying for mercy, for our government's magnanimous detainment. The minister's line is . . . he can't remember not doing anything. Then he has to go to question period. Then he has to tweet righteous indignation. In a flash the foreigners are loved, so his strategy goes accusatory; they've accepted Iraqis, so put that in your sweet pipe and—The should-fights will go on until election day or the boy's image is forgotten, whichever comes first. The dinghies sinking off so many Mediterranean beaches won't not wash ashore, those babies lulled dumb by sea kisses. Oh, you woe-peddling poet, if Canadians already with you look upon this verse, what else, they'll ask, can impassioned, reaction-happy fingers click to make our petty country leaders give a damn? Witness. The clamour will away. Do not ask so much about this emergency that the power brokers' names get scrawled on the hearse. But let your love be driven to witness: home is the country stolen and infiltrated; home is a country of "migrants" who stayed. Land lovers tell stories that we, wise world, should look into. Your moan for a drowned moppet echoes the drunken enmity this country settles with, meme after meme, wishing blame gone.

72

Hole was the mother, fucking. Women smashed. Pennyroyal tea drunks holding out for rupture. Loud substance, a fuck-you for teens to recite— what mess, a pre-Ritalin smellivision, a neediness murderess. Alt-bitch beauty contusions. Housewife on ludes. Love, after Grammy nods, after Kurt's death—dogeared Love is on the floor, getting media requests. Little Frances is in *Vogue*. Prove your authentic pop-metal contempt, affect a high-energy nothingness, swore the nineties. Apathy approves the tuneless melody of fucked-up. Washington punk grrrls dated peevish boymen whose fuckboy mentality trivialized grrrls' true hardcore sound. Sleater-Kinney and Bratmobile do more for me now than mainstream frontwomanned crews like Veruca Salt did—I was innocent, awkward, hanging around more popular party girls who threw up on boyfriends' records, who teased Rollins boys with ambition. Niggaz barely registered in the truth-wound of plaid thrill-will; Fishbone's singles played in campus late rotations but let's face it: Olympia's revolutionary sluts were acutely pale. Overanalyzing grunge may seem false, but its nevermind ethos informs the anti-sympathy humours of today's hipster disinclinations. Its alternative to the spoiled, makework eighties rocked *Billboard* but felt meaningful and true—or maybe my nostalgia just remembers Bikini Kill subculture with more foreshadow than it deserves. My body, having dissociated the anger Dickless expletived, had faith no more but could thrash shame in mosh pits. No one ever mentioned riot grrrls' lyrics to us, lines full of rape gripes and mock slut-shame. College douchebags played 7 Year Bitch's anti-patriarchy CDs while coercing frosh virgins; bros being bros before there was a name for such dudes. How shocking that we could be yelling that loud, yet be so Lovelied, mouthing screams like sweet nothings we weren't worth.

Tradition has it sonnets' aims are to glorify love, and lovers. Then how must my forays into these lines make us beholden? When I originally conceptualized this reclamation, Will's leavings were just source, just canon fodder for my fearlessness. My war-like, dominant hankering set upon those poems' boughs a weight, inch by inch, to reshape and fork their meaning for my gain. As I grew stronger, they complied more baroquely, like ruined chords disintegrating into ornaments of a wealthier melody. My rumination shooed the sweet birds that sang in meter without listening to their song. But the letters William arranged are hard to fully subjugate; their characters stand in the way of my acquisition and sway the foot of my verse. An unsettled feeling, unassimilated into this ethical understatement, pushes a Western wherewithal back into my hand. Invisibly and visibly the black ink is ghosted by doublethink. But a kind of love is at work, I say, in dreaming this second Shakespeare, a love for the same poetry even supremacists love, a superlative idealism in linguistic form, and a sadness written in me by those who dumb Shakespeare's tongue to english their glorification of whiteness. A gut love for those who fuck with conformity's unfairness. The admiration that I once had for Shakespeare's ardor for his youthful dotee has been altered by my experience of stalkers, consent-hounds and entitled male attitudes: those bullies who'd write chapters extolling my virtues and enumerating my faults totally expected their obsessive, consumed state would be my compliment, when they in fact were charmingly breaching my explicit, drawn boundaries. Now a hundred and fiftyish dedicated billets-doux seems a creepy *and* literary achievement. These sonnets hold out hope for a collective sonnate —a word-heightened, choral morale—that sparkles patriarchal, objectifying love into a new game, where your beau sends you this verse on gchat, soliciting your affirmative consent. A love that well-wishes without object, that honours the muse this dark lady hears above verse, below song.

74

Bruh beat be like, content. Dude docs like a white man. They material defence. They all arresting image. Without jail colour. They bail on a sistah. Verbally he open carry. Metrically he waaay money. He collegial. He frat. He hide that. Fresh bling glint in his line. So women show interest. What sick hos cry for? Bruh Modest Mouse. Bruh Reddit. He all startup-illest wit. Bruh beat push teen liberals. He all downstay. White men brutha. Tom uncle creepin. Nice-view penthouse hints. Pimpin this thought. He do Slit Review authentic voice. They a sorry party. We-ain't-those-conservatives cred. Mo fortunate. Mo totally humane. Cachet they can't earn. Hood they can't have. Big butt earnest. Bruh whip—cha! Institooshion his dude. Homey spirit dist-ill. He interest held back. Net interest pay smart. Negro formal up in here. Software hawker inta house. He badness. He stabness. Gut love his stunt. He doctor the register. Officer the reallife. Brother pretty can of worms. Memory body be indyin. Nigga deal dope theatre. Who coward? Who conquest? How offishall written? Scratch hip hop sonic knife too base for infrastructure. Who feed to be remembered? Brother worth short shrift. He attention seeking. Rhythm aint sway here. White choir master content. Aint said no damage. Brother aint stupid. Bruh wisegame this landscape. Bruh beat his unwhitewash. He hustle a hardcore. Core remain stone unsaid.

75

So the air I give in poetry, consciously, to my thoughts, is as a safe room dedicated to allowing. Strife disorders balance; verse is sweet syllabic therapy, a physio of mind; a stretch into swollen resistances. Percussive talk is tapotement to the grr ground by microaggressions' tone-deafness into my rhythms. Maybe peace of mind is fantasy to my journalist's apprehension, and lyric the destination utopic wishes strive for, move earnestly toward. The unwritten text, a promise, a realization still dreaming. The disavowed health of whistleblowers effloresces in the soundproofing. I didn't know poetry could be a space so vulnerable; the joy of feral privacy; an inside anonymity more profound than doubt or knowing. The filed caches, the impressions of language, the witness silenced, live in this restorage facility, this short-term erasure of now to account the infinite. Managing best to be with my interlocutors by being alone, I still hope I can better our world. That the world may be served by my pleasure, the somatic letting go into meter, heart all full with feasting on homonymy! Here endurance sits tight, and by and by the clench relaxes and the starving tenderness is fed. I would trade it all for a loving kiss, but for now poetry is foster home to my surviving sexiness. Growth and art's productive urges require surroundings conducive to delight, a place saved for what is soft-hearted, or else making is just fear forming a new body. This room, this bubble of temporality and okay, is the disabused bodymind's emptiness and disillusion transformed back to itself, day by day. A turn toward regular things —to my nieces, to walking. To surrender that allows the strain to fall away.

Why is my verse? Am I so barren of a normal person's work impulse? the inner good girl asks of discipline. Sonnet never ventures far from her unvarying preoccupation with here. What sort of quick thing is a poem? What kind of change? Why with the time I have do I not get a real job, or at least freelance? On the far side of the round table is the wife, the prostitute, and the mother. Why would the rational mind choose—demand—to compose? What unwinds so strangely in the line? Why do I write line after line still all on one topic, ever the same, and keep inventing reasons to bind Shakespeare in other-gendered weed (threading as though every word's a grass to braid)? A verse mouth almost tells my name, shows my breeding, breathes an heir's birth. Handedness writes here, as does a mathematical eye denied due process, an education knowing its unwilled illegitimacy. Love, I always write of you—the land I try over, the purposeful land alive to violence, land that resists my innocence. All my argument with sonneteering, all my best effort, is in redressing old words' indifferent power, suiting paternity in unrecognized skin, regenerating England's Canadian, brownish, phantom limb. A secretary, a lawyer, and a head of state parley in whispers at the round table's front. The real Sonnet, who wanted kids, was shunted into this productive fail. My role is inconceivable. My want's bastard unfolds. So is my loveshed still telling what firms wish untold.

That crazy inning's rollercoaster thrills will be rehashed over brewskis for the rest of time. How the Jays broke a slump of over twenty bittersweet years to make the playoffs; the division series at 2-all; how twitchily we watched precious minutes seem to waste themselves on nervous plays. Score at two and two. The ball leaves the Jays' catcher Martin's hand—a simple throw to Sanchez, interrupted: the white ball hits the bat, held up like a spar in the left hand of the surprised batter, Choo. It flukes down the third-base line. A man runs in, ignoring home plate umpty-ump Scott's upthrown hands: time out; dead ball. Mistake, right? The run won't count? Banister raises a stink; cites rules; weirdly the umpires confer: the run counts. Thrown tallboys, garbage and plastic cups wing from the fifth level. The unruly crowd shows off their badmouths, pissed. Gibbons raves. Only when little children get quivery, the horde remembers decorum. Play on. Three-two for the Texas club. Suddenly, they drop simple balls. Shortstop Andrus's bad day becomes our team's leg-up. There's a man on every base. Toronto's forced to know time's playthingly, devilish progress to eternity. Look what the whimsy of the game summons: a frenzy the crowd can almost not contain, as Andrus commits another error on the base-crowded flare Donaldson tapped. Ball players on two sacks. Score three and three; two outs. Next at plate, that firebrand Bautista, who strikes at the first pitch. Midfielders fidget. Dyson next hurls one down and outside; ball. Jittery observers send mojo from their jumpy brains to Bautista. Dyson looks, throws—José cracks a new anecdote into our shared colloquial inheritance! Outfielders watch it fly mutely into the stands. The slugger flips off niceties with his wood: the flip that breaks the internet and Toronto's bounds . . . Jays will take the lead and division. Sports hacks have a field day, waxing lyrical prose on the drama of it. The Shakespearean drama, they write, was such as men swear epic in those mythslinging poetry books.

The son of the father vanquishes the villain; the values spoken in undertones heretofore, now mighty: multiculturalism, liberalism, a blonde wife. Don't misunderstand; I'm much relieved, less fearful of this heir than his predecessor. A critical stance in my verse was evidence of my contrary, alien penchant to that government; my words could be used against me. Order under the Trudeau theocracy will surely return poesy to its sponsored position? Poetry was once the nation's keen mythbuilder, the stuff that taught the dumb Ontario high school kids to sing Acorn. Today what earnest verse can stay the ignorance algorithmically grafted into our flag-flying psyche? What kid grieves Canada's debt to Sacred Feathers? In Toronto the liberal aura now reddens the right wing. I wake and give thanks to unknown grace that Canada's troubled majesty's government might yet be most proud of its Charter. The lines which I compose can register less war-whoop, less policed influence. It's two thousand fifteen, is the comeback from the golden child, born of the father, who includes mothers and wows dorks. I've been the brown mug for do-good leftists before; my trust wants mending, with more than style and nods to the arts. With defaced faith I try to answer to the poet's grace and sing the braced heart's belief in the boys' clubs' better natures. I ohm Cohen, saying Joshu was a rapist. I ohm Duncan Campbell Scott's inflictive masculinity, articulating Canada's id. I'm those boys' meritocratic ideal, my self-governance as highbrow as Literature's. How now, Justin? How savage are my rude designs on your inheritance?

Googling "white peopling," I stumbledupon proverbial anchor babies
defined by Urban Dictionary. UD should call me queenpin for I pwn
thespian terminology. The attitude my verse asdfghjkls is sonetic: phonet-
ics and virtual worlds' porn aesthetics alloyed in a gentle sonnet's grace
—in a butterrace's kinetic, vowelful, embodying phrase. Ragealicious, this
numbness-cure, this sick overshare. Opensourced, the dictionary records
slang trend; my sic-liking Muse digs other thugs' ill vocabularies, but
the anti-other bullcrap there is blah. Once I was ignorant of sweatermeat,
oblivious to cleveland steamers. But a hype girl who overanalyzes hip
argument deserves the TMI of urban verbage, so now I feel trill, know-
ing queef, safeword, ratchet, sapiosexual. The angry pirate, the donkey
punch. The twats and haters of the internet are shady poets who drop
THC-inspired vocab explications. Entitled thirteen-year-olds' bs theses
come from handed-down pornspeak. Forty-somethings thirsty for that
teenage affectation thief lexicon from databases that explain therian, lac-
tivism, freegans, and truffle butter. Why is Urban Dictionary so white?
Who stole that word game from the Dirty South? Bad archival behaviour
betrays the uppity diction tacit in the epithet "urban," and gives bomb-ass
tone to definitions undesirable to certain moms. This is a white-boy's ass-
cheek; he can afford to urban-down, to praise thot, pedo staches, trouble
butter—to toy with argot so inherently unwhite-collared. So is the lyric
verse game a set of aesthetes robbing thankless but authentic minions of
their street flavour. So this attention-whoring bad bitch crashes your squad.
Pomes with more issues than *Vogue*. Bye Felipe, I keep saying, to the dirty
sanchez, strawberry-shortcake economy. To the so-woke folks, this queen
throws truthy self-care dope. Stop and smell my gloss.

Old friend, how I fail some responsibility when I of you do write. I don't know if, through writing, a better spirit will lead my troubled thoughts. But these days your name agitates my mind. I think of the pranks we didn't scheme together, the stories of misspent youth we didn't share, the girls'-night laughs we dissed as unfeminist. The thought of your contempt would make me tongue-tied speaking of my loser infatuations. Now your happy family life is the bull's eye I never hit. You're still setting the example of how to embrace your worth. Why didn't I learn the self-respect that you modelled in adolescence? It was self-fashioning, I see now, into white womanhood. Me, bumbling along, never able to sell my overfaithful reproductions of a damsel undistressed by race. Imbalanced from the beginning, our partnership assumed an easy, surface posture of scorn toward prettybaby strategies taken up by intellectual inferiors. We were young feminist assholes—but you refusing a small-town beauty championship is not anything like the sour grapes bravado I cultivated to make believe appearance doesn't carry weight. You wilfully appeared sensible; you skirted any slur of shallowness and yet held the power of your high school laurels. I wanted fate to hold me up to a fairer light; I told myself that I would achieve loveliness through talent, not makeup. Ambitious us, brainy young girls: you'd undo legal chauvinisms while I'd rewrite the popular headspace. Of course there was no weirdness over boys, no competition for guys' wooing. We were too jacked on academic accomplishment to waste our worth on mindless boy-attention, right? So while I fought off routine assault, boys walked you from building to library and showed off their good sides. Sisterly, protectively, you said I chased the wrong kind. The fish in the sea threatened me, but my thirsty vibe was asking for dishonour? Because it was a way to hope the worst wasn't true, we shamed me instead of white supremacy. Will we now survive a realer view, that pretends no mystification wondering why love came to you?

Not rising tides, not changing climate, nor soil pollutions vex me lately. Who could register pollutions of the particulate physical, or turn toward matters of lake acidification, while their psyche doubted its own survival? I feel, when I think of Earth, that my greenness is rotten, my feeling rotten. My heart is meanly disconnected from you, friend, whose memory doesn't foam with toxic agitation when another story of Black life devalued pulses through our consciousness. In me each particle weathers the racial real. I bear it in my flow, in the underground of my attention. Your environmental alarm feels familiar, like someone's whisper of injustice, like a fact implored by mortal flesh. This flesh can't feel alarm that doesn't drive through the protective anodyne regulating my concern. My care is gone to the social, to tolerating the world as murderous atmosphere. What died in me is the earth; I can only yield so much to the oblivious culture. The petal of common feeling trampled over and over. Whiteness is a way of understanding the body that numbs when faced with its own melanin; its eyes are brainwashed; my petals struggle in that light. Lately my composure can't compose an unraced environment. Is it selfish, that the central love object of my gentle verse is the nerved within? I cherish a sensibility that questions the ownership of propriety and property. I create sounds in the behavioural wilds of terrified adults, and trust that song tunes territoriality toward being. Say your breathing shapes language into culture. Hear silence when all the breathers of the world are white or dead. My environment touches me; what kills the empathetic cellular kills resolve. Such virulent communications of race hatred must be filtered through my pen. I sound brown where breath most breathes, and intervene in the green mouths of men.

Ingresses. Places on the surface through which insertions of thin metal. Current of qi. An education of my muscular voltage. I am open-ended. The centre of my forehead, a meridian, an eye site. Awake in the soul circuit, I attend to attention. The practitioner looks at the needle's delicate medicine as working on the body's network of light; I channel writers like Rumi who speak of the primal root. Filaments quiver in my skin; I am recumbent and objectless. My bare legs are pin cushions. I give over to energy, laying back in the soft recliner, working through a restless animus. My fontanelle firmed over the Chinese knowledge that finds, at the meeting of hundreds, a fountain of nadi, a convergence of vitality's pathways. At my wrists: the outer frontier gate, the yang valley. Yin metropolis beneath ribs, just past my spirit seal. Shining sea at the ankle. My body thrums energetically, forces that are me are stimulated by the gentle force of tradition. I sleep. Wikipedia says acupuncture reviews find no long-term benefits to short-term treatments, and that researchers studying sham pokings find the effect of implanting placebo needles is just as therapeutic as the "real" thing. Could the rubaiyat of saints' and doctors' souls be proved canny? Its poetics weighed in lift of heavy hearts? The nerved head's activity responds to what astral touches rhetoric or prick can lend. The pharmakon of puncture could be as airy-fairy as watercolour, as abstractly curative as Miranda July. My vibe is sympathized with ancestors by acupuncture's unexplained work. Lodestones body empathy with my intersubjective flesh; the metal quills inquire like good friends. And so the instrumental register of a sonnet's pain is a thing. Something unhitches the believable from belief. Channel gutter, cubit marsh, jade pillow: the regions of channelling, like chakras, where needles plumb bloodless lines. Three pins stick out of each of my ears: thin, metal, Buddha-sounding.

Rain forest verdant. Sawtooth-edged salal at your hand's height. Drops of jade glinting. Now green cut diamonds, there, underfoot: water droplets. Rosy pussytoes push rosefeathered white tufts from green florets. Pointed alpine firs, just rising above coastal forest, stir. I found, or thought I found, my own understanding in the viridian exteriors of the unceded. The bathmic, subarborescent tenderness of a poet's mind is equilibrated among the dendrites that green here. Forests have instincts like global positioning systems: to walk under their report to atmospheres and satellites is to you yourself become instrumental, geotactic, sexed with plants. Narrowleaved owl's-clover, maiden pink, arctic eyebright: Salishan knows their information well, far better than any modernist quietude will. Douglas water hemlock to Douglas maple to Douglas hawthorn: a forest translated by botanists speaking of worth. What worth there is in you, Douglas can't English. You grow in this unrelinquished silence, the fronds of your mentality synching with the aspen colony, its underground idiom, sprouttongued. White spruce, shortspur seablush, Sitka alder. False bindweed, common rush. The forest's glory begat Hul'q'umi'num', a language dumb foreigners misheard. My interpretation of rain forest says *beautiful* by being mute, or whispering: *i ó e á: .* Leafy liverworts, downy veilworts under cloud. Light drizzle veils the cliff fern and brings out the malachite green of mossy branches. The forest lives more life with me in it: one solemn life, walking the territory of resource fairy tales. *I ó: e* , say the plant brothers to scraggy consciousness. *Larix occidentalis,* is all our poets can, in rival praise, devise.

As I ask who are my kind, the commission's report tells where I am. It
says most explicitly things which covenantees said before. My "we" forms
in the work to meet the calls to dismantle the dispossession. Canada, your
multiculti child can't praise fathers' abuse, systems you alone are guilty
of. I hear ninety-four bids: One, fewer children in governments' care.
Two, collect and publish findings, yearly, on kids in the system: Métis,
Inuit, First Nations. Three, use Jordan's Principle. Four, set the standard
for woke laws on child custody and apprehension. Five, help young need-
ful moms and dads. Next, repeal criminal protection for schoolteachers
who use force and get a strategy to reduce learning and work inequalities
between Indigenous peoples and the rest. Answer the call for the elimina-
tion of poor-relation funding for on-reserve study. Within that pen that
endorses legislation is the duty to write annual detail on the education,
accreditation, and income achievements of will-not-be-subjects. Lend your
jurisdiction not to the state's small glory, but to justice, such that she that
writes of you can quit fighting the Canada-myth-machine. Culturally
appropriate, healthfully oriented curricula—Treaty-honouring legislation
—will dignify this exercise. This listener's search for community listens to
calls propping higher-ed-meaning Aboriginal students, for toddler educa-
tion programs. Country, what in your language is writ must acknowledge
right means people speaking Indigenous words, preserving what nature
made so clear in the lands' languages. Fund such an act as counters the
trespass against first languages. Inshallah, Canada. A fundamental ele-
ment of this country's wisdom: tongues and idioms, talk in Gwich'in, in
Naskapi, in standarized syllabics. I hear a call on feds for a Commissioner
of Indigenous Languages, recommended by callers, devoted to reporting
on the adequacy of whatever money or support feds put toward fluency.
Colleges, universities, be places of reincubation. Help school survivors
rebuild the family names stripped from them, by fixing status cards, iden-
tity papers, documents, and passports—for no fee. Maybe get tobacco for
an offering first, from now on, so dads don't embarrass me? Do it for no
praise which raises your profile. Make amends as actions I can body, and
live a respect to relations, to elders, to words and circles.

85

If my nation exists, it acknowledges that the upheld health of Indigenous persons in Canada remains in defiance of previous decisions made by Canadian governments. Residential schools were a gross decision. Health rights, says international law, are rights. Indigenous peoples and communities want reports on their fight against injury, addiction, and suicide; reports on available services, child mortality, chronic ailments, and psychological conditions. Off-reserve health concerns require an approach. Aboriginal healing centres hold wisdom for those carrying old residential school consequences; Aboriginal healing practices need precious space held for them in the care system. Basically, all the medical and nursing faculties should be filled with Indigenous kids, and young doctors should get real-schooled, taught to serve with skills attuned to residential wrongs intergenerationally borne in bodies. Twenty-four bids to action: childlike, I believe urgency lettered into settler culture will work to listen an "us" for me, that will allow truer cultural memory. Calls affirm the independent role of the RCMP to investigate crimes (actually establish a policy) where government interest might be at stake. Better limiting statutes, provinces, to ensure no limitation defences are afforded those whom Indigenous peoples might prosecute for historical wounds. The formation of lawyers should involve a course on conflict resolution, anti-racism ed, and cultural competence. Hear plaintiffs' allegations fairly outside the previous Indian Residential School Settlement Agreement. Too many Indigenous people are in custody—alternatives to prison must be given support. Let trial judges waive mandatory minimum sentences. Sponsor the most pressing of priorities: fetal alcohol spectrum disorders. FASD offenders need compassionate correction. Allow healing lodges. For inmates who remember abuse, treatment. For halfway houses, support. Listen, who nations so many youth in custody? Enough victims—track who gets victimized; log violent offences suffered by Indigenous peoples; fund victim outreach. Enough women murdered and missing—welcome the inquiry: a demand to stop the violence Indigenous girls face. The treaties remember the handshake between European forefathers and nations' foremothers and forefathers. The breath of those words awaits respect. Governments, defend Aboriginal justice systems. His majesty's dumb thoughts still speak lingering effects.

Forty-two actions I knot into this hopeful procedure, as mindful plant, sub-
altern, refertilizing the space of the English language's breath-taking verse.
Bound up by the very craft with which it tutored my breath, Shakespeare's
apostrophizing now props challenge of fairness. Fully adopt the UN dec-
laration on Indigenous peoples' rights, I echo callers, into weathers of us/
you. That declaration should frame strategy for reconciliatory practice.
Work it through together and issue, on Canadians' moony behalf, a Royal
Proclamation of Reconciliation. The proclamation will forsake excuse-
making concepts like the Doctrine of Discovery and *terra nullius*. Recognize
mutuality, re-establish Treaty relationships, reconcile treaty law to minding
Aboriginal law, hold nations partners in Confederation. Affirm the yearn-
ing to redress—in writing. Write a Covenant witnessing this spirit, thereby
furthering the spirit of the Settlement Agreement. Unlearn thought that
overwrites Aboriginal sovereignty. A moral and spiritual pitch, that social
justice groups and churches get karmic: Indigenous self-determination's not
determined by God. Neither He, nor his Ancestors, sympathized with *terra
nullius*. To build equity, create institutes of Indigenous law. Publish gov-
ernment legal opinions involving anything impacting Indigenous claims
and treaty rights. Governments, adopt legal principles that accept, when
occupation has been established, the Indigenous claim on territory. Once
that title has been affirmed Aboriginal, parties calling for any limits to title
rights are obligated to say why. Form an oversight body which monitors
progress on these post-apology #goals: a council, established in com-
pact with Indigenous organizations. Endow a National Reconciliation
Trust with the funding it needs to advance the cause. Provide the coun-
cil with information it seeks; report formally on the "State of Aboriginal
Peoples" and the advancement of the cause of reconciliation. Also, edu-
cate public servants on Aboriginal history. (As if I was not already sick
over my fathers' constitutional bigotry, my fathers' Catholic trespass on
First Nations tires my Marguerite-Bourgeoysed heart: hear testimony of
children, of remembering adults, breathing white men's unholy actions.
Our Catholic guilt isn't repentance.) Families call directly upon the pope
to issue an apology. They invite the Vatican to declare how their servants
weaponized Christ to break families' bonds. Apologies matter: the con-
gregations must listen and feel their own troubled ministries.

87

Faith leaders—Jewish, Moslem, all the other church parties to the obligating, signed settlement agreement—form young priests, rabbis, imams, or ministers to respect Indigenous spiritualities, acknowledge Aboriginal wisdoms. Explain to faith workers that residential schools were church wrongs to be righted. Churches should work now to establish permanent churchly funding for projects that animate community-authored education, healing, reconciliation, and leadership in Indigenous faiths. May the worth of Indigenous perspectives and teaching methods be confirmed at all educational levels, by requiring mandatory learning of Aboriginal knowledges and accomplishments, histories, and legacies. In partnership with Aboriginal elders, develop a comparative curriculum in Aboriginal spiritual beliefs for denominational schools. What good does reconciliation hold for -ers and -ees? Let researchers be supported by the country's granting bodies to advance understanding. For youth, let the state's riches go fairly toward reparation, toward youth networks establishing community. Deserving is not the issue; the cause of this call for action is recognized. Affirm: the mettle of Indigenous communities isn't wanting. And so let museums' policy be patiently reviewed and backed by Aboriginal-institutional discussion. Answer the call for reserved funding, this 150th anniversary of Canada's self-mythology, for museum grants vested in deconstructing the colony. Own up to the worth, the truths, King called "too-inconvenient" knowing, ignored by library men to whom the country gave its archival stewardship. Recommit, else mistake your calling, to housing holdings that testify to the great wrong of residential schools. Fully adopt the UN principles Joinet and Orentlicher surmised. Provide records to the Commission's agents, coroners, and slow statisticians on Indigenous children's documented deaths. Establish, develop, and maintain a death register marking residential school student deaths. Establish an online registry of cemeteries, plot maps that judge where kids' interment might be marked. Inform Indigenous families of the burial locations of their cleaved children. Honour families' need to rebury the deceased. Maintain, document, protect these evidential cemeteries, deferring to the most affected families in each matter. Into survivors' knowledge, keep asking, but when asking, know *no*. Know who breathes the xxxxx of so much silencing shattered.

Any "we" I want asks archives to identify and house residential school material. Let ten million be disbursed plainly over seven years to Centre directors, so they might manage restitutional doings, with extra given to research and record local place memory. Governments, work with communities on just heritage and history: a reconciliatory framework includes commemoration. For Indigenous representation on the history sites board; for criteria, regulation, and practices of the National Program of history and commemorations; for a heritage plan for commemorating residential schools—this fight. A national day would prove, in public theatre, the government's sincerity about Indigenous histories. Honour struggles with monuments; honour children parted from families, survivors, the work of Indigenous peoples, with monuments, in the hearts of towns. I can heart wherever I hear calls for work by Indigenous artists to be financed; or to get Aboriginal and settler artists acquainted to team up on just behalf. Heartily repair the nation's broadcaster, so it can set down a story of faults unconcealed, and of Indigenous diversity, wherein #aboriginallivesmatter. Aboriginal Peoples Television Network—word that this worthy labour continue, and let journalism institutes and good media schools teach Indigenous style to writers. And much glory to Métis, Inuit, and First Nations athletes. Canada, by supporting the Indigenous Games, will be a gainer too; for getting behind Indigenous athletes helps community health. Love old-school Indigenous sport and think about Indigenous athletes' inclusion at each level. Let no host country invite injuries to territory in the name of international competition. The business psyche must check itself: Indigenous rights and doing business aren't hostilities. Development requires real consent, fam. Indigenous people need opportunity and jobs; truly effective managers will be trained in Indigenous rights and anti-racism. Information for newcomers must include histories of the many peoples who survive this nation-state. Revise the Oath of Citizenship, so that belonging to this nation is founded on affirming the treaty promises that gave breath to Her Majesty's legal claim. Ninety-four calls I echo, overweaving acculturative song, looking for my neighbourhood, in this weather of the Commonwealth's speakable wrongs.

Raised on fairy tales with beautiful, innocent heroines, but denied credibility as beautiful, how could I be rescued? Wait to be kissed, wisdom whispered, wait for some faultless Apollonian boyfriend to notice your winsome smile. Let him comment upon your charms without taking too much offence; let him speak of masculinity's lameness and of his feminist reading habits. The right man will win your heart with litigation against the patriarchy. Reasons make some men disingenuous; so in your defence: the man you can't resist is not the one you love. Demonstrate cis-girl's grace, let men half your size dominate small talk about your expertise. The right man will form your superheroine fan club, organizing desire for the radical change aesthetics you'll someday sell for disgraceful bank. Let innocent white women get trophy-wed, your skill is willpower. Acquaintances will rape you and you will strangle hatred and look at the strangler's beauty; you will be sent away from the pretty walks and interiors of matrimony; the good man will guess the hymen-sweet beloved name that no man before has hallowed. Well. Lest I too much profane the idea of romance, I should explain. I don't think courtship is wrong. And the apex of human interplay, scaled through the fore and surge of libidinal acquaintance, is also poetry's swell. But for this sweet marriageability there is no hero. I've supported myself while listening for the vow that would be worth tipping the balance I've cultivated. For my bond I muse and wait, and never love him who demythologizes husband, but doesn't undress hate.

I bought a house on the Island. They gave me work at the university. A house! What will I write, if everything is okay now? Now what will I yell at the world? Instability lent my words a careening drive; I sat down to compose my ruminations; the straightjacket of this knit with what Shakespeare writ settled me down as I flailed at fortune. Now I make money. I bought what I wanted. I don't know how to dream without the opposition of the force that trained me after loss. A house! Doors, windows, laminate! When I listen, my heart asks what a house is to me: a brickshaped trophy, a working-class sorrow, the comfort-zone we inhabited while glancing rearward at our frauds? Someone's conquest (turned into owning-a-house) forgiven now, tacitly whitewashed by friendly financiers' deeding? What I earned was financial, systemic, borrowed against our lakes and air. Under the ground where the house sits, beneath the stolen surface I purchased, are exploitable minerals; Canada's government keeps the rights as the Crown's. If they want to put a new pipeline beneath my lawn, they can. I have met the conditions for the lenders' approval, which makes me a citizen at last. How can a homeowner feel othered? Petty griefs may have done their spite, but I made it into the belonging set: I am welcomed by insurers and home fashion retailers. Suddenly my design taste matters; finally I understand the way everyone else worries. We fight off fortune's might, and other strains of woe, by owning something. Choice words now seem woefully meagre compared with the potential loss of this centre. Poetry will know its place—its emergent properties—from now on.

Some granola mothers hype eating their afterbirth; some fashionistas hate any uterine discharges—I'd kill for some more time to menstruate health-ily, for that red wealth some, still in their full body's force, wish over. From the first elementary school reddening of undergarments until thirty-some-thing, I ughed at each month's new femaleness sign. I bled unmindfully, as if just forgetting menstruation's rhythms could free me from birthright. My awkward stance around bloodhounds, around some men who sniff iron in the air, and some who presume anyone who doesn't moon over their manly humour is "having their monthlies," wasn't deliberate. I just never could pretend to please; nor could I pretend womanhood wasn't visceral. We bleed iron into fibres and soils and jeans. Someday a body will value the minerals vested in our blood product, collect and harvest the par-ticulate, and resell our discarded fecundity to us. Intimacy measured me menstrually: the stained white bedsheet; the boyfriends who negotiated penetration while bleeding; the sisterly traffic in heavy-flow narratives and discreet, beneath-the-stall femme-product handoffs. Yet youth ignored what birth was to me. Birth is channel to these words, to humanness. I wanted to channel the proud cycle of birth; I wanted to grow little arms and legs in my uterus, but the costs of my control-freak defences around little-girl bright sides were steep. The want of children was weaker than this ambition to embody the force menses became in me. My desire to have children was a strength ceded to fostering an ideal. All lone women's pride I boast, not wretched in this aloneness, but channelling that birthing code here. Tumours materialized my combative hystery. Eventually the dark resonances of anti-Blackness in sexuality—held in flesh—hardened, swelled, and bloodily announced, in red-soaked garments, my lost war. My omectomy floods the bleached market.

Little boy, I'm pushing to adopt you. I'm here, forty-two, reasonably stable (stable for the first time maybe ever) while there you are, shunted from family to family, wondering what family means. For the first time, I might make of this life something given. You aren't yet assured mine; your mom hasn't signed any relinquishing and the foster mom has known you longer than I have. The reality of love is about who will stay. For you, reality depends upon the adult you're with. Love, professed without discipline, won't help. Right now you need kin who can edit their own fears, who know that the worst of wrongs can live in what's left undone as much as in the horrible abuses. You don't know your father; your mom's risky life has taught you fear and lies. I believe a better state to me belongs than that which you've known with your mom. My humours do tend to the depressive and anxious but I have fought to contain those energies; I out them in poems. What vexes me will touch you; my inconstancies will matter; this mind's conscience—its habits—will inform your lived, felt notions of sane- or batshitcrazy-lady. Reactively, I've isolated myself from the gaze of masculinities. But you will be that gaze; you have participated already in a boy's title. God, the irony! I must find a happy honesty, to have it to share with you, to love you the way a principled mommy ought. A boy needs belief in his responsible future, needs exactly what's missing in my home—a noble, responsible role model of masculinity. Raven, this situation forces me to see my father's nobility. I can adopt more than you; maybe I must adopt new belief in adulthoods, in a maleness anticipated by the little child who will know my edited, underlying devotions.

93

"Space Oddity" shall live on, as long as we live. Ziggy Stardust's purpose we'll sing: the young art fags, the trans lucent ladies, the king bees and ballet dancers, all grieve Iman's dead husband. The hard world saw love's face in that glam space cowboy—what he instilled seems like love to me —as though starlight chose its ambassador, and descended into the world to become a physicality of love rock soundwaves. Bowie, the messenger of the galaxy's heart. Goblin King, Terry's brother, Placebo's fellow, rebel: the personae can live on. Lover, even the hatred in The Thin White Duke's "nasty character" is there for exaltation. Theatrical, plastic soul, your American pantomime struck an odd chord. With your changeable interpretation of masculinity's looks, your metallic threads and false eyelashes, your sartorial flash made music history. Your wit is writ in the mood alterations and freak show stylings of later bands: New Order, Pink, Lou Reed, the Pixies, the Smiths, Marilyn Manson, Lady Gaga, Queen. But now Heaven, having lit thy creation, desires its giddy ashes to ashes. Super creep, earthling pirate, labyrinth monarch: your face wasn't sweet, but your melodies and grooves synched remote musical worlds, brought Neverland to New York. You still sell, whatever they thought of your sort. Patriarchy's heart is working; it still beats chaps with your looks, unless they own a Caulfield, Lanyon, Basquiat, and Hirst. Sing, then; dance the blues—boys, it's a sweet thing that dies and still survives in the astral plane. I hearted Bowie for loving a dark-skinned model. Even though his Somali spouse got explained as just another queer sympathy, a Black beauty is the songwriter's widow. What if the young Americans were to virtually realize such transcendence? Bowie, starman! A comet bursting white unworldly show.

Earthquake. Say earthquake. Earthquake. A little shiver with the power
to hurtle land masses. Little wiggle of geological destruction. Oceanic
earthquakes tremble down below; tidal motions, heaved by tectonic hot
friction, moan and surge; they do most damage to shores when waves
behemoth. Moving motherfuckers, earthquakes. Earthquakes. Metaphors
of selves as stone, unmoved, crack; even stoics get ruffled when hard
ground torques like soft toffee. We tempt fate who live on the Island.
Out West they rightly advise, on street signs: *here, tsunami threat*—above
an innocent stick figure who races to higher land, the big wave curls . . .
But it's the Island's nature to shudder; it's crisscrossed with seismic faults.
Under oceans, moving expanses of mantle shift, rub continental shoulders;
every day, imperceptible earthquakes flutter through roads and towns.
North America is a plate of earth, stacked tectonically over Juan de Fuca,
which pushes down beneath the Western coast. A subduction zone is
what we're in, with Washington and Oregon. The Duwamish, the Hoh,
figure u e i —the Comox, Cowichan, Quileute, Tillamook, reference
u e i —the Yurok, Makah, Klallam, and Alsea stories e e a o o a e i
i o e ee a u e i (Ee u a, a a a a, a uea) o e a e i a e. The
Huu-ay-aht, through stories, e o e u a i a e e e e e i a i at
Anaktla, Pachena Bay. But believers of European data did not get why this
subduction zone was so peaceful, until they started following up a forest
extinction near Washington, then begot the Japanese an inferred seismic
mom for their "orphan" tsunami. Earthquake. West Coast earthquake.
Knowledge base of naturalist witness, centuries-old document borne in
surviving narratives. u ii! Looks like we're due for the Big One, sixty-five
years overdue. A silent wave will set the dogs barking. Then things will
turn shaky; houses will lurch, bridges twist, buildings fly off their foun-
dations. Then the ocean, elevated, a five-storey wall, will swipe us right
off the map. This Friday there's an emergency drill. We'll fearlessly review
drop, cover, and hold. The website teaches quake, tsunami, wildfire, and
zombie preparedness.

How sweet is a long run under slow evergreen! The smell of yew does things to the soul, makes the psychodramas ebb. White spruce soothes like anaesthetic; painkillers in the fragrance of trails. Forest bathers dope themselves with phytoncides, snort the beautiful myrrh of the anodyne buds! Depression gnaws me, but outside knows a weathered heart. A sweetness dose waits in the outdoor pharmacy, assuming I can make it outside. I get enclosed in my thinking head, with its fleshless tongue that tells the story of patriarchy and dismay, that loves making classifications and envious comments. Prisoner of autobiography, narcissist, poor thing, it says, who cannot distinguish praise from butt-kissing, who seeks a kind of love in praise! It loves naming names: the enemy's and mine, the same. Bless the sane chill of fresh air! Phytotherapeutic woods! What fragmentations and flagellations have those voices wrought that won't, amidst white birch, reform? The tall firs' habitation—like a cathedral's cloister outdoors, said the settlers—is where bitterness can submit to greeny scent, where vulnerability gets a stand's posture. When shame covertly hormones my very bloodstream, and all things turn my story to unfairness and threat, my eyes can't see steadiness or likeness. When dread, dread, dread leads my heart, I must wrench to the forest, where its pulse can recharge my sense of privilege. The hardest work isn't the versifying. It's the pill-less acuity I choose, the live edge I don't varnish, lest I lose this edge.

Some say that it was a conspiracy, that fault lies with Grayson for plugging that bitch's dorky game, that the wanton Quinn traded ass for good press. Others named Sarkeesian as harpy they'd most like to disfigure. 4chan psyched itself a lynch mob. Touting ethics (ahem) in video game journalism, trolls made extreme sport of bombarding their fellow gamers with hacking attempts and threats of assaults. Gamergaters loved the idea of a feminist conspiracy. The image of vindictive, plotting feminists hatching "communist" machinations (not in smoky rooms, but in the lefty, vaulted halls of disgruntled academia) to destroy macho gamer identity motivated haters. They resorted to harassing women, giving the finger to safe space. They profaned the *Depression Quest* developer's name, gutting her basic sense of safety, doxing the "social justice warrior" so that she fled her own domicile. People bullied Wu as well, suggesting if she had kids they'd be murdered after she was choked and raped at her home address. Even a year later, tormentors continue hating, sending Wu their fantasies about slicing her genitals and defecating into her mouth. How can such ruthlessness be translated? Anonymous douches will forever troll forums, expressing things they'd never murmur in daylight or to a woman's face. Always flamers will abuse comment. The images of hate: what cliché! My sonnet suffers, repeating such worn, flaccid fabrications. No poetry can lyric lifelike a bully's ambition, or metaphor the feces they would have us ingest. Literary books can't translate hate's boring words. Manly gazers play games, fight realist fights, shoot virtual people. Cheerleaders are welcome, especially if they count as women the industry loves. But developers without penises wield the strength of virtuality, like leviathans boys are trained to behead. Brutality does not stop the girl-love that, like a feminist pansexual Cthulhu, rises from the subreddits. As Yuggoth sprouts its zombielike fungi, the minecrafty feminine rises; Mother Hydra games oospores into the wet dreams of *Super Mario Brothers*.

Hooboy, what a hellish week. Give me aww imagery: kittens in knit-
ted radish hats, charming baby capybaras wrestling celery from bunnies,
kittens in furry costumes that disguise them as purple koalas, furry cos-
tumes on ferrets that style ferrets into little ferret-lions. Gifs of capy-
baras wearing cowboy hats, ferrets squeezing themselves beneath doors,
attractive penguins fearlessly twerking their tails, knitted pairs of socks
unhanding a panda. Tiny human babies are also effective: I can aww hard
at two-month-olds dressed as caterpillars, metal babies rocking Sabbath
"Paranoid" onesies, babies-as-green-vegetables, wary newborns who peer
out from Batman swaddling. Give me baby ferrets this time curled in
palms, or venturing blindly from a water glass; give me tumblrs of lambs
tenderly nestled with micro piglets. Show me tarsiers emailing, auks stum-
bling, bichons growling from their rich moms' Birkin carriers. Please, that
I might bear in good spirit the ways entitled old men unburden themselves,
post gifs of athletic Black prima ballerinas' sick jetés, winding women,
more winding women shaking booties as feminist intervention, the epic
eyerolls responding to some dude's ceaseless oratory, the talk-to-the-hand
flips, the *Ab Fab* duo slurring dahling, the First Lady asking: turnip for
what? Beyoncé's made *Lemonade* out of some men's bunk; let her Black ops
meme hope formations, however ephemeral, into my social enduring. Some
fathers' dominions feel ruined; support for some trumped-up troublemaker
ascends. The image's pleasures wait on them too: here's Obama in pho-
toshopped thobe; here's unicorns and rainbows ironically photoshopped
over a hyperbolized Bernie Sanders. Dems and Republicans don't mean to
unite over tiny baby feet held by muscly Adonis-men, or gifs of dalmatians
wearing antlers. But there's something about a dressed-up llama; it cheers
the absurdist and believer. To save myself, on loop I'll keep playing that
sublime video—where around the living room glides the cat, wearing the
shark's fin costume, riding a roomba.

Looking for someone fortyish. You must have a responsible penis and a boner for consent. Looking for the inspiration one gets when a person understands poetries. I do appreciate mindful dress, but don't go in for a fellow who is terribly impressed with brands. If the universe put a spirit of calm in you, that might balance the verby thing in me that lights sense associatively; perhaps you, taciturn, will laugh at my wordbrained leaps. I'm down with him who enjoys contemplation over theological essays, nonprofits over business trips, and a discipline that honours the sweetness inside himself over a sacrificial love that feigns indifference to infidelities. (Oh, whatever it was in the gods' humour that enforced a Canadian childhood with no crushes uncoupled from attack, I've charmed it. I can actually envision consummation of my desire to desire. I've mastered the storytelling that foretells successful romantic choices. I'll try again.) Person, you are still as envisioned and hypothetical as a poem still unplucked from the immaterial world. One has to learn to hear subtle harmonies to confidently go after new fusions, no? Never yet did I talk with anyone I could hear: I hadn't yet listened to me; the limen of soul to body's voice was choked; my disconnectedness only heard false praise ring true. The deep reverberation, the humiliated groan closed in my apartheid-crossed legs: it thundered under every word I ever spoke and rumbled under my attempts to know men. But a quiet—in me born of gut-fight, the guttural unrest, spoken —I found it. It flickers, like a light. The quietude, the raw sunyata: from there I now listen for you, you pattern of thralls and thoughts and genital history. You: patient, responsible, freak. Me: as down with wine and oysters as poutine, likes walks on the beach and youtube aww vids. Equally as comfortable wearing a T-shirt and jeans as Byron Lars or Duro Olowu. Sense of humour: dark. Kids: how I wished. Athletic-ish. And except for these crosswords, I don't play games.

The first story I want words violently thus: why didn't I, as a child, know these sweet neighbours, thief? When via race did you steal thought, steal empathy, disrespect the Two Row Wampum agreement, fathers? Ancestry smells iffy in Tkaronto; misinformation mutes my loving elders' breath. The purple pride which on patriarchy's soft cheek is no foreign complexion dwells livid in my colonially versed veins. Settler history taught to me was whitewashed—the truth too grossly dyed with blood. That pride relied on a bully's selective conscience: Germans deserved damnation, apartheid forever damned South Africans, but my hands, I learned, were clean. Bullying Canadians were not found in military journalisms; they hadn't stolen a thing. My history class taught Vimy's victory was the birth of a sense of our sovereignty, while fathers were fully aware of the original peopled spot on which our claim did stand. Someone's child refused blushing red with shame, another won a white-knuckled fight with despair; and they whom authorities recognized nor red nor white heard your story of unstolen. Not far from Brantford, the Six Nations, just down the road from my history lesson: but they could have been on Jupiter. Nobody ever mentioned the Haldimand Tract; no one explained how the treaty breathed went broken and unwritten; how for their service, theft. An Indigenous man's pride, if spoken of at all, was mistold as xix xxoxxx xxox a xexxexux xaxxixax, ox xxixxixe xxixixixe, ixxo a xeaxxaxxe, ixxexxexx xuxxexx. Just up the road, the Six Nations were sheltering memory from settlers' false education; I wrote answers in my notebook. Already I suspected a citizenscape little Sonnet couldn't see: a bullied hearth sweetness, a neighbour colour, an authority had stolen from the storying of we.

C

We whispered to our aspiring girls that they couldn't become U.S. president but that they could forge paths to the Prime Minister's Office. Our sisters longed to speak of the woman President, and now there is a chance that gives us all the feels. Hillary Clinton, first lady to use her First Lady might to step into the Senate. Methodist kid, athletic girl scout whose early fury sprouted when NASA said women weren't worth the lessons astronauts get. She dared be keen on a high school presidency; got told of her stupidity to think girls had power to lead. She had canvassed for Barry Goldwater's presidential push, had studied subjects in the light of Reverend Martin Luther King's unforgettable dream. Freshman Republican, she mulled and changed her straight-girl side to Democrat as, at Selma, in gentle numbers, voting-minded marchers crossed the bridge and as wily spincrafters spun a Southern strategy pleasing to the racist ear. Classmates voted Hillary first student to speak at commencement; the ovation for her oratory of "the possible" lasted fully seven minutes. White privilege and unmistakable talent compounded to give legislative Hillary's pen both skill and argument. Bill recognized her strengths, her appropriateness, as beauty; they embraced a useful matrimony. Did love's sweetness, or surface, survive their trajectory? His infidelities meant Hillary's private annoyances were public inklings—many grown women would have been felled there, ruined not just by his faithlessness but by his infamy. He became satire's object; she moved house to Chappaqua, New York, and embarked on her senatorial métier. Kids' defense, progressive health reforms, 9/11 responders' support, women's rights, the Medical Leave Act, LGBT rights, diplomacy in the world's theatre: she's got drive, a Grammy, and qualifications. I'm not naïve; she's far from perfect: Obama she's not, but kinder than Thatcher. Still, where only men have walked, this mother now steps. Her life has brought her to the cusp of presidency; she invents her story, and history. Grandmas cry as they bring granddaughters to polls. Black girls look at Michelle and think past president's-wife.

Sometimes altruism just can't. I make excuses. What speechcraft will bear the puny amends I make for not checking your neglect? Boy, family, this truth isn't beauty: the ideals we glorify in videos and books are ideals. The truth of my aloneness and the beauty of my autonomy are forms of love scraped up from the pioneers' dominions. Your aloneness echoes the wrongdoings of colonial afterthought too. I can't do it: your mother remains indignant and still defies the needs your apprehension cannot make her answer. Your gramma is blind to abuse and will not admit what she has taught you. Into the intimate play of ignorances that is your truth I intervened; a single woman of colour walking into a shitshow of skipped breakfasts, contempt for child court, sugar fixes, drug abuse, authority issues, random epithets, french fries, plastic bags of pissed laundry, conveniently stretched truths, trips to Walmart, agency battles, toy guns, YouTube, comments within earshot of "would be best if races had never intermixed," barbecue chips, arguments over who knows what he needs, inconsistent praise, whining, *Call of Duty*, lost rechargers, "you'd better," dumb excuses not to call the social worker, and cries of outrage about *that woman*'s lies. In the car on the way to Brampton, you asked when you could live at home. You talk too much, you said, quit talking. I have a gilded solitude, a room of my own, a baby grief. You need a network of neighbours, two parents, an annoying sister or dumb brother, family friends, grandparents nearby. I'm still learning not to be the tragic heroine. What I don't have, I can't give. Now my office is the room that I used to think you'd take; I teach students young enough to be my young self's kids how to make thesis statements. Raven, sometimes on long drives I still hear you in the back seat, singing Lukas Graham's "Once I Was Seven Years Old," because you were.

My love is intersectional, aware of things white women don't live and men don't go through. More weak I, brown girl, might seem, because my emotions range. Emotional overseers want emotionless thought; the less colour shows the more enlightened I appear. That emotional oversight is a flesh merchandizer's demeanour, the judge's—whose patriarchal esteem rationalized owning slaves, the owner's—whose tongue pronounced vows then pushed between the legs of his help (who were very well behaved for monkeys). The code of stiff-upper-lip, of exquisite control over weeping, was a New World manner developed in the colonies, but was it plantation whippers or skin-stripped pickers whose emotionless gaze was worth emulating? A man I was sweet on just went wild for this girl's "even temper." Such beatitudes for a white, motherly woman's steady, level-headed ways. When has she ever processed the bodily vomit-repulsion vibes that hate cultivated for my mother's figure? How often has she stuffed down the rising self-defence and stopped sullen her breathpipe like a xixxex? Show me the neurons firing, synapses every day signalling notice, notice the ratio of the skins, the unmarked vs. the marked: *tag,* you're *it.* Run, defencelessness, run! Isn't life more pleasant now than when the person's mournful hymns did hush the night, than when brutality tamed that wild music by stringing up runaway threats like skins on every bough? That woman's administrative sweetness is grown on common decency. Only some humans calibrated their demeanour to defer to enlightened- and defend against alt-whites. In the real forum of flesh, unlike here, I sometimes hold my tongue, because I would not tempt the decorum bully's prosecution with my song.

A lack of listening, what poverty. My muse has been some abstract listener, imagined by a self formed by fear and competition. I thought that having an audience was communicating. Who are you, person? I can't open long enough to show you the respect you deserve; I'm trained to hear the argument. Meanwhile, you're listening, and I'm barely noticing I'm heard. Your presence is of more worth than whatever I'm saying. Listening has felt like humiliation, but you make attending into grounded praise. You're beside me, not blaming anyone, not mentioning any petty thing friends said. You're in motion, recording interaction, writing it in your heart. When I listen, this book isn't as necessary. The "our" I've been seeking, the place I've sought, is here. And there, where you are, "we" appears. You have faced the ego that overgoes my blunt invention; you quietly embody the human propelling my lines over land. I'm so busy doing my best, sometimes I disgrace the very witness my furious witness intends. Your intentional listening, fount of calm. Our togetherness calms this striving to mean, this drive to ungrammar the Western subject, this heart believing itself alone. Your trust is the reward, if I listen well. Fellow, person, what do you need? Opening to another person, all the defenses my verses serve soften. Don't overthink it, you say. Listen, soften. Your graces and your gifts dissolve my urge to tell, and there is more, much more space, here, in listening, than in the aspirations my verses speak. Can I sit by you awhile? Can we be grounded in your knowing? This is the last poem; I just want to shut up and open. I want to say nothing, human, when you're right here looking for listening.

To me, you were a freaky, fairskinned father figure of song. Uncensored lyricist, your naked verse caressed my unnubile, ten-year-old, deflowerable ecstasy. How young we were when first we heard of your eye caught by Nikki masturbating in a hotel lobby. Aphrodisiacal purple synth chords, electronic hymns to funk, your androgynous beauty lashed titillating, throaty sex at nuclear winters' and cold wars' threat. A little red Corvette drove me from the conformist interests of schoolbooks into the Revolution's love manifesto. I hummed verses of "Purple Rain" as I developed breasts. The mixed-race, liquid-gender vibe, the auteur-pompous sparkles and rings topped charts. Funky fellow, pre-autotune imp spinning turntable gold, you inspired sensuous excess. Pop rock father, sugar daddy, my innocence was lost to the sounds of "Head" and doves crying. I seduced a girl in the recreation room of her parents' split-level: bubblegum perfumes, pink skin, thrilling tongues—soft, wet, hot juvenilia. Madonna's crosses burned; her sinfulness commoditized was our first fetish; meanwhile your fresh mouth was horrifying rich-mommy-and-senatorial-ballbuster Tipper Gore. Parental advisories hadn't yet happened; your "filth" was labelled vulgar by purity police; kids learned to dig albums authorities branded explicit. Stealing from Little Richard, Curtis Mayfield, Marvin Gaye, Chuck Berry, Elvis, James Brown, Stevie Wonder, and Bowie, at a pace hyper would call hyperactive, you dropped so many tracks your label sweated. The unpronounceable symbol which became your thing (on your cheek, "SLAVE") frustrated music journalists lacking adequate font for the-artist-formerly-known-as. A soundless glyph as the artist's name was contractual insurrection. Masculined feminine, eyelined manly babe, decimating categories of groove, defy mortality! Hush our fears of life-without-Prince. Shh, fears of this opioid-strutted age. The Purple One vibrated at a mauver level. Pleasures of you were born while he was. His bedroom, a butterfly sanctuary. Man, a sexy motherfucker's dead.

Let not my bardolatry boulversé be called la misanthropie. Ces billets douleureux ne sont que la trying de ma colère qui voix my beloved dans les humains. Idéologue, moi, asking how, since all qui ne sont pas les premières stakeholders doivent sonder complicity, our songs and praises peuvent betterer. O,   , personne, proofer of sonnets! What   will parole us, autochtones and developers, from kind discrimination? Poesy loves tongues, son son, dada sympathique, ohm un sorrow for unkindness instillé par des consonnes habitantes. Extinct arawakan phonologies drop chupses dans ces expressions de cellular Résistance. The lip-service Reconciliation manufactory, l'aversion de my verse. Mon patrimoine est ce   , this standing Canadianicity, colonial fusion cuisine force-fed. Ma langue misses its   origines; British Singhs express raj things; later Rupi Kaur braves about difference. "Fair, kind and true" en anglais: cette équivalence de pâle et juste, cette homonymie (dit mon argument) de "fair" est unkind et untrue. Les vainqueurs écrivent history, les pas-vaincus write   . J'ai besoin d'other words and listen to other words pas les miens. Survie-stitched language is my invention, Shakespeare comme ouï-dire and lettres of here threaded entre thèmes de fils. On stolen land, je tresse origines with origins, like the ceinture fléchée woven by my dad à l'École Rivière Rouge. Pas-Métis, moi, I'm cope AF, for a kid métisse franco-indo-afrikain qui body Canadian truth. Sorcières have often lived alone, where their cultures hate and heart them, leur sagesses trop for nationalist lore knowers. This writing, ces vers, sont ma   ptsd-ing un mixed-up   en sonnet.

I work light greens and pinks into the chromatics. Now light coral, sea-foam, soft white. Abstraction like diluent, muting my intensity: I see roses, not red. Eggshell colour, I palette variations of the fairest whites and beiges, with touches of Athabaskan pale jade, watery beauty making beautiful golden rivulets stream metal in pastel greens and light blushes. Soft celadon lines undulate amidst water-green; muted lovely pinks line light strokes of brightening thought. Sea-beryl crystallizations of sweet blue-emerald acuity spark above striations of blush and lavender cloud. Bluff of cloud softening into soft light pinks and soft greys. White smoke wafts membrane over white isabelline, then rivers an antique periwinkle wisp through fluid shapes of light verdigris expression. Cascades of waver-ing streaks touch aurora borealis into my nursery-bright quality. A rosy colour makes eyes at tender green. Now soft pale light brushes chirpy stars into airy, rose-starred blur. Glint of pop rocks! Phonetic squigglies! Gold flirts with pinkish colour. A stipple of mint green spirals coolly outward. Pinks and light greens, figureless, streaming and unformed: they look like ideas but with divine materiality. Greys and whites in the underlay, threads of bone ivory, softest pinks visible below. Evenness of luminosity, green of honeydew, colour worked into the tonal. Sing, formless wave of wishful being, of chroma. Now behold these purples, magentas, dark yel-lows. Whorl of dark violet that eyes return to, from wonder. Then blush-violet, then lavender, then chalk-toned green diffuses to a pink-green opal, iridescent blaze.

This was not unimaginable to my brown fears. Brown folk grok the prophetic soul of the wide world, which downstreams white dreams banking on things to come. Now uncanny poets breathe please into the foamy truthscape: a slough of voters glommed control; the not-supposed-to have seized the pen. The civil sheen forfeits its command of our military, complex, offshore-industrialized doom. The immortal moon watches Earth-weather eclipse itself; undercurrents surface. The comedians and the sad augurs mock their own prescient, cynical guesses; insane certainties now crown themselves; we are assured a brand of peace protest cannot sully. Last night, we commoners watched as our livid selves peeled back the skin off an endless rage. One by one, win after win, the states clothed themselves in red. Shocked reporters read off the figures in failed emotionless tones—in a disturbed calm, stunned by the unfolding cataclysm. The enemy was suddenly us, those we loved, those who look like us—the fresh wound to nice ladies' psyches, the death of their comfortable superiorities —as liberals cried, liberals saw their own race. In spite of him, we will have to live in this poor version of America, while he insults history and principle, roaring dull and fatal speech. Something elected this: something tribal and scared, something branded and thugged. How, multitudes, can we, in this unreality show of alternative good, find each other? How long, Liberty, will your monument stand, when a tyrant's cronies boast of civil liberties' ban? Poets drop their f-bombs in dissent, while official-lipped brass bands air-kiss the next Best President.

Watch out for fake poetry. It plants ideas in the brain. It's shape-think. It may fake the character of woo, so deep, but this phony speech hates the right knowledge. Its figury attitude to the correct mastery of true spirit whets stupid sympathies. Real news is for us to speak. Whinewashers don't know how to register right what may be expressed. What dummy says love? Or says that daydreamers merit anything? Nothing, sweet boy, that them dharma bums try should get likes. Say prayers to divine right, for we must each day, over and over, assert truths every schoolchild has to memorize. Counting is a chore no one should worry their nodding little heads about. Only losers distrust chief officers or undermine their authorities. Fake sonnets, fake villanelles, even fake-ass uncreative writings threaten America first. I am hallowed by true poetry; it hails my fair name, so that I am eternal. In Loserville, in Loserville's freakshow cantos, poets weigh words, trying to be great when they can't. They don't understand that real poems compliment power. No jury or fake judges can order gifted verse writers to tone down. They will not cease to mark the anniversary of this winner's win. The fake poets' little protests please the cucks and feminazis, but make no sane thinker quit glorifying fucking glory. The ayes have it, as they're paid to. Great poetry gets financed for flattering the first lady's company with great conceits. Fake poetry for losers never talks about my heart: it's huge and big and red. Everyone knows my heart is sometimes so American it's devastating. True poets show my heart steadfast. Only criminals would show it dead.

Pokémon evolution promised transition: Bulbasaur's morph to Ivysaur, Squirtle's change to indigo Wartortle, Charmander's flame-led rise into fiery Charmeleon. Spearow trained its short wings until frightful Fearow's beak manifested. Green Caterpie shed itself to become hard Metapod's chrysalis, so Butterfree could one day emerge to quiver dance and flutter toxic fairy dust. As easy as Meowth might ripen from money scrounger to jewel-foreheaded Persian, our transformation from immaturity to something more powerful. We crushed on optimistic Ash, on Iris, Cynthia, Misty, or Brock—on Serena in her straw hat. Their friendships—boys with girls—trained our battling hearts. Unsupervised for many hours, we mated monster fellows, inventing offspring off the official inventory: Kangaskhan sexed Lickitung to make Shlickimum, a threatening mother salivator; wily Ninetales did Forretress's bumpy protrusions and gave birth to Ninjunk, a steel-plated fox. I caught Shelmet, Vileplume, Noctowl, Poliwrath, and Growlithe; I caught Grimer, Exeggcute, Chansey, Gyarados, and Ferrothorn, aiming at mastery. As they levelled up, Clefable's Disarming Voice grew more accurate; Furfrou's Charm and Doll Eyes dazed more attacks. Such "feminine" manoeuvers I bred into males like Volbeat or Throh, so sluggers like Hitmonchan spritzed Misty Terrain or Twinkle Tackle upon their foes. Creatures' reified genders felt fictional, like fluid performabilities that could be substituted or changed at will, like kinds of damage. Boy- or girl- state, about as random as Ditto's shape—that's how we played it, coding our little mods into the Pokefranchise. Pocket monsters of status legendary embodied sexuality, but as nonbinary and genderless, fantastic and normal. Like a vulnerable female Victorian, exposed by quaint home botanizing to natural plant hermaphrodity, was I queerly informed by Phione's form. Last July, Googlers searched for Pokémon Go more than for internet porn. Gotta catch Pikachu's yellow-tailed devotion: that universal, electric, animal pull. See you at the convention, where youth transform into sexy Umbreons and sexy Nidorini—at the location augmented with characters made up by the real world.

Alas, I still mistrust the mirror. The days have long gone since they, fresh-faced playground youth, described in painful detail how I made them puke. My young self hearted their Motley Crüe affectation; they reviled the brown dog who tried to be a human girl in their group. When I look at old photos, their ughs don't make sense: I was lovely, with delicate hands and a ballerina's posture (we all had eighties hair). Models now trade on caramel shades of skin like I rocked. My offence was obscure but irrefutable. Ineffable, but actionable at recess in the raw gravel. My worth was no better than urine, they interpellated. I was the piece of shit that kids have to look at and construe as filth. Some ran shrieking; some wanted to cleanse their yard. They washed their brains of garbage like my body until my body was humble, grateful garbage. They're over, these troubles, aren't they? Why ache a saga every middle-school yard will rehearse? Didn't my francophone father, in his youth, withstand much worse? Each second, some fratty superdouche somewhere voids his butthurt on the sparkle of dreamy babes. After school, full of venom unwillingly swallowed, I staggered home, wondering how to save what was being methodically killed. Does cruelty have no end? Am I pestilence? I asked my imperfect parents. Intelligence is never welcome, growled my father. They will degrade you if you don't dumb down. So my insides were as repellent as my brown out? —a fateful thought, a pretty mental situation. My body had learned to perceive itself as grief; now my mind was bug. I looked in mirrors, looking for the version to put down, the one to amplify. I amplified a confidence in words, as though speaking could give me welcome into exclusion's heart, but my poems whisper the garbage visions they forced down my throat. This poem isn't my best side. Too heavy-mental, ha ha. Sonnet, when will your poetry figure out that your endless moaning about this stuff *is* the unlovable thing? Hatred, I break into a sonnet.

Hot-formed lady shake she donkey. Sweet brown sugar twist she behind. What for a tune, chile, if not dancin? The Mighty Sparrow he mek yuh wine. Little gyal goddess done teef men's eye. She got a roomful dem peepin she backside. Hot heat spreadin down onto she belly. Wet heat from her form mek a boy loose tie. Female form provide the action. In public, sweetmen answer she smile. Child, public manners don't mek batie less round. Female body drive the dance hall wild. How come yuh sittin when yuh batie so poom-poom? Yuh nice amerindian friend gone come. She give Sam Baksh reason to dance. Dhaalpuri, pattie, and a bottle of rum. She dance to Mighty Enchanter "Dulari-Beti." She swing to Aubrey Cummings's lead guitar. She dance to Colin Wharton; she work The Saints. She like the dum dum duddy of the Telstars. Shanto song body the spirit uh Guyana. Mek the Indian tap and white British mind. We no more under England rule of law. Down yuh colonialism! Rattle yuh behind! Like a kwe-kwe is dance hall be jumping. Partiers plenty high wine will drink. Portions of chow mein, souse, and dumpling. Latrins' steam counksy, rass strong stink. King Fighter, he bounce up wit Lilian. Roaring Lion mek sly observation. Better nah marry pretty-ass one. That girl will mek fuh bitter union. Thick dunk woman devour double an pepper. She dingolay; she dance calypso an roll. If yuh not erect, best expect correction! Pity men think she under bai control. Gyal friend, bacchanal does be bouncing yuh backside. Tsk, yuh tek your eye and pass me? River Corentyne heart, your serpentine twine. Yuh is enough to cuss—remember who yuh rass be!

Your long, overbearing disputation of my point is so manly. Do you try
hard for the impression of a filibustering lawyer whose prolix speech strives
to lull its gathered listeners into capitulation? Or do you paternally bestow
a lump of wisdom upon my brown forehead? What do you care if the
W.H.O. calls me when a pestilential terror of ills imperils a country? Or
if I am the number-one deprogrammer of enemy backdoors? My knowl-
edge need not obstruct your discussion of the shallow clichés you heard
somewhere. Men like you, all over the world, understand that I must strive
to know my shames and praises from your tongues. No one else has ever
explained that to me, I intone sarcastically, but you don't hear tone. It's
actually riveting, how oblivious you are to my interest level—no, it's not.
You think you'd sense my four attempts to change the subject away from
"the no rights or wrongs" of dating students. Into the profound abyss of
your egoism I throw attempts at dialogue, at mutuality. They career into
the gulf between you and others' voices, where your apathy for my address
transforms, in mid-air, my generous responses into criticisms you blank
and to flattery you hear. Your ears are stopped with arrogance; your mouth
could use a cork. How familiar with the manly neglect of female input am
I! Since I got regularized, I now dispense with the expected, pretty defer-
ences. Your attentions are not so strongly in my purpose bred, that all the
world besides methinks are dead!

Stinging cells tip the tentacles fringing the polyps' mouths. Family to sea anemone, hydra, and jellyfish, corals live in many-minded masses, anchored to hard surfaces, growing together in sync. They grow over centuries, agglomerating into reefs by secreting exoskeletal calcium carbonate under their derrières (or, they poop the architecture of their limestone foundations). Cities of Poseidon, Nemo, and Marlin's apartments, Ariel's geographically impossible kingdom, these ecosystems house species, offer hiding places and habitat. Sea turtles, puffer fish, clams, octopuses, snails, jellyfish, groupers, and parrotfish orbit the colonies' stony forms. Waves deliver little animals to the lethal nematocystic fingers, but dinoflagellates symbiotically residing in the soft flowers of coral also eat light and spew photosynthetic shit down the coral hatch—so food happens to sessile reefs. Quietly, coral reefs ate plankton and built themselves into majestic infrastructures. They are a tenth of a tenth of ocean floor— where a quarter of all marine life dwell. Even tropical rain forests cannot brag of such biodiversity. Clown fish need mangrove detritus; sea urchins need spiny lobsters. Surgeon fish need dolphins; a shark needs a wrasse. Human appetites need fishermen who need their catch. Foraminifera need the same water quality as reefs. The temperature of the world rises; the oceans warm. The gentle balance of symbiotic algaes and pigments shifts. The microbes' hosts' water heats; their favour for their resident life forms ends; the corals expel all their colourful, friendly zooxanthellae. Tendrilled mountains grow pale under the shallow sea. The display of colour now blighted, the corals look white, like forests affrighted forever. I cannot shape a metaphor environmental enough to say our fear. Our nature is inescapable; our fear morphs into new forms; people write and write. They say Fabien Cousteau is making polyp homes out of the substrate natural coral use. He's making man-made structures they can use—making limestone skeletons, via three-dimensional printers, for underwater worlds to use.

I'm not sure whether it happened in Manitoba or Alberta: *go home,* they complained, *go back, wherever pakis or niggers come from.* Was I seven years old? Was I five? The day was cloudy; there was wind, and a sidewalk underfoot—a path of cement on which we kids marched. In whose place was I a guest, if home wasn't this flat territory we were on? The hard sidewalk under my shoes; their sense of here. I walked home alone—I say "home"—I went where my parents paid rent, right? Our house wasn't ours? Overhead, the sky spread out; the sky's country was itself. We had moved from Ontario, but my gut got that they didn't mean there. Immigrants, all of us, we'd chorused in assembly—the more immigrants, the kindlier the country, the folksier the mosaic. First the English and the French, then Western Europeans and the Ukrainians, I guessed, then Chinese and Indians, then the Guyanese and other such Commonwealth stragglers? Eventually we'd bring into "us," Canadians, a panoply of the human race—so my sweet young self, in Trudeau's aftermania, believed. Those children's hate had a kind of guilelessness, however, that conveyed my abjection straight from their Canadian parents' hearts. I was foreign to clear distinctions between master and savage—to fantasies of homesteaders who, by subjecting trees to their saws, had "mixed their labour" with "unowned" lands. Homesteaders, they called themselves, by principle: "home" was theirs, because they were first to fence it. As if we still were at war with whatever made entreaty against their fencing, my existence existing too near threatened. My very being entreated something before I ever opened my mouth. *Get lost!* Here kingly kids drink from institution's cup. Something older than English yea well knows what with his guts he must disagree. Something français dit bon, histoire-là, je parle au-dessus du poète: domination, Dominion, domicile, home. I protested: one of my parents is here's occupying family! Don't blacken me! Please see my colonists' blood, inside! They practised the policing of reserve on the surface of my brown skin. They practised homing in on enemy. The clouds above, the sky above, witnessed. The land underfoot said, here was here first. We thought about beginnings.

After the election, I slept. Lines that existed before, that progressives wanted credit for eradicating—colour lines—became visible even to those sheltered white democrats who said Hillary could not lose. Survey says you, dear white granny, sweet white daughter, unbosomed your judgment to pick this new administration. Survey says not only white trash said *yessir!* to stirring enmity. Where I work, it's almost fully white folk—academics and scientists who live university lives. For days afterwards, my face burned: my classes saw real fear; I proffed a brutal reckoning. In the meantime, women (whose millions of votes, like hands held up to an oncoming accident, did not stop the car wreck) began preparations to march in Washington. Elisabeth texted: voluminous women! Stand with marchers in Washington, Left Islanders? Hmm, Vancouverites? I was busy, shaking off Shakespeare writing "tan sacred beauty" to mean beauty's loss. I volunteered to nothing. I went to my parents' for Christmas. More sleep. Slept. I have always had good intentions to divert strong minds from capital's Barbies to the course of sensualtering things, but alas, Whitmanesque poetry my fear did not assuage. This shock, of the immanence of unabashed tyranny, I mitigated with television, food, and internet. But when every channel says Now Racist Global Overlords Defy, YouTubers don't know if they mean they did or we should, and nothing is certain other than uncertainty. I cried. I tried disowning the present, and doubting everything, and officially fucking the rest. Holiday over, back on the Island, back to Elisabeth I tried writing, *no.* Try as I might I could not say so. I had to give fuller growth to that which instills solidarity with others, to that force which forces us to grow. I said I'd organize a thing in Nanaimo.

I googled "protest" "march" "successful" "Nanaimo," to start. Not much there but a demo against Harper's omnibus bill agenda, over four years before, that had attracted a few hundred like minds. I called the name on the internet for help. Though I was a complete stranger to Bill Eadie, humanely he spent a slow hour giving me the insider-to-Nanaimo organizational 411 over the phone. How hard could it be to plan a march? We had all of two weeks. But I'm a solitary person. When I demonstrate, it's in literature my passion finds comrades. Can't I be in undies, with the comforter warm over my thighs, while plotting the rhetorical moves of decolonial love? Nope—it's impossible, alone, to be a movement. The national girls fixed up a march page, on Facebook, that looked profesh; I downloaded templates for posters. And I sent an email to university folk, hoping for takers: *stand with women in Washington? Help!* Susan, Cait, and Kathy rose; Kathleen, Eliza, and Janis rose. Every woman's deserving of basic respect, said knitters, whose needles' worthy industry plunked pink knit toques on women all over the world. The pussy-grabber's hoggish hubris had roused a sense of right, not to be taken down without love's fight. Nanaimo's a forestry town with miners' foundations, box malls and a quaint harbour. The girls have rosy lips and cheeks from walking the hiking paths. Wives bend in yoga classes; rock chicks show tat sleeves at local boys' jams. I played shitty acoustic guitar at the open mic so I could tell the collective about our apolitical gathering. Susan got wicked shirts; Kathleen did tech; Janis' boyfriend fashioned fonts. Bill rustled permits; Cait wangled food; Kathy wrote press kits; Eliza brought amps. I was responsible for leadership curation, for whose truth was the event. Eleanor spoke the lead, gave thanks to Creator. Rose's friends, old-school marchers, lifted their voices, beat their drums, offering woman-songs. Defiant under the pavilion called Maffeo Sutton, proud Valeen fucked shit up— we listened to the voice of growing resistance. One thousand marched in Nanaimo. We marched as one movement, as the world's women moved.

117

Messianic child, muse maker, Lithuanian Polski, Montreal Ashkenazi. Your father in the grave, you scooped an old bowtie from dad's closet, cleft it in two, buried one of the severed wings in a shroud of longhand, in the yard. "To see your thighs and start weeping": Lorca's words electrified you—teenage seeker, heart searcher—and altered your path. You forgot shoulds, let poetry enter your dearest longings, allowed the universe to call you sorrow's hero, pleasure's troubadour. McGill's bro bonding supported your apprenticeship to meter. Dudek, Layton, MacLennan—the boys' club knighted you, bard youth, as part of a fellowship that strove to be free of the Queen's rhythms. Beautiful women without hangups, who bucked convention, who had their own minds, made the turnt parties you'd give. You wanted a persona: intimate, manly, brooding at führers, tugging a raincoat on a wet night, held by dearest purchase in ladies' hearts. The night that Joplin perchance gave you head—you hoisted it into song, into an immortality, into a carefully smooth, dapper wink. Shrewd, you saw Hank Williams called the Hillbilly Shakespeare. You learned chords could transpose a poet's tax bracket. Money wasn't the farthest thing from your mind, but your songs suggested sex might be first in your book of longing. "Bird on the Wire," "Sisters of Mercy," "Winter Lady." "Famous Blue Raincoat," "Chelsea Hotel," "Suzanne"—each ballad, desire-driven, scored for seduction. Your low tones made tea and oranges sound so juicy! Songwriter, you proclaimed that profane and sacred fires burn as our manias and heartaches. Liturgical—your music, your literate, bare lyric. Knowing myself within the level of your fraternity, fellow minstrel, I observed your poetry's sexy hosanna, its prophet margins. Your spiritual quests, your meditations, your work to waken, your dharma of aesthetic deliverance—were sincerity, robed in masculinity's charming appeal. I saw you at Rogers Arena, and I did strive to suppress my competitive vibes. Now, hallelujah. "I love the country but I can't stand the scene," you said, and died—leaving *Saturday Night Live* to dance us to the end of democracy and your love.

Will those who like a pretty sonnet fathom these takeovers? Some of our appetites are more keen on witnessing the ephemeral graces, on recording those moments of poetry when beauty undoes us, when our predictable attentions surge into an *attending* so acute, we become open and reverent —to shadows of lilac on a cupboard door, to many particulars of a sandpiper's scurried x's in the sand, to wild geese calling out our worldliness. Romantic keener still, I also wish to commune through the sublime, that magnificent Blackness glimpsed when we ponder our being—to see our neverendingness of being, full of everyday cosmos. But I never needed that much Nature for transcendental transport; yet I sing a sweetness to heal a bitter state. Must I convince us of how the occidental outdoors were claimed and framed by pastoral imagery? Do I offend by tending and befriending poets sick of welfare verse? I found a kind of sublime, an extreme of language, in this palimpsestic experiment. I am blown away by the mind, by its bodied arisings, its order amid entropy, its human limit, its other shapes—walrus, citrus, virus. Perception itself, heady trip. Just being with an arbutus produces lyric philosophy, if you're into raw love moved to language, if you can still your consciousness to empty non-duality, then pull the stillness into word. "They'd rather hug a western cedar than hug a homie," said my Latinx friend, of greeny white folk who'd refamiliarize us with maples but stay estranged by skins. "I" am the nature Nature made, the Darkness made by binaries, the thought an epistemology named wild. I am the i u a i colonists *Lauracea*ed amid Arawak's healthful state—whose "wild" speech a rank of English others professed. "I" need a gestalt shift that would unboy philosophers, and unwild all subjected to that slur. Heady, but then cedars begin old time storyin. Gyal, Europeans wanted to find their way back from a Fall. They scienced their story so it was untrue. Cedars laugh. Strong poetry, that science! They scienced ownership too. They mythed what we so-and-sos knew. We unfallen. Then they called themselves "poets"—those Romantic keeners, those Fall-antidote seekers, like you.

Would I have tempered, or lowered, my expectations by now, would I have said "alright" to unremarkable wedlock, if my satisfaction rested entirely on an extra person in my bed? Instilled in us from earliest memory was that boys followed their dicks, they'd eff any opportune hole. Male desire was a hormonal hell within that propelled yearning, fearful advances that they could barely hope to restrain, and we should hope to satisfy. Our fear, then, was of being unsatisfying; we learned to call our satisfyingness what we wanted. When I saw myself wanted, I'd gotten what I wanted, right? What wretched errors we make when our want, the myrrh between our parted thicknesses, isn't ours. Many matrimonies close upon untested water, depths her own fingers still startle from. I was twelve when I heard that a thirsty boy, under covers at night, could slake that thirst himself. So blessed was I with penis envy, I wondered how I might brave my own cravings, how the want that honeyed me should be taken in hand. Touching, first, the ingress, a part—here was a betweenness, specific, not quite inside, what skin, touched—my fingers traced a question of touch, inquiring. I quested a maid's shuddering, feverish O! but spent myself until I tired of spiralling unknowns. I'd fall asleep. I then decided to pursue depths, to penetrate, to not beat around the bush, but to probe, insisting my body answer to vibrators, handles, stiff vegetables. No luck. I made better moves on myself eventually, and learned a fecund, independent love: now I whet my own appetite, satisfy my own urge to starburst. I thrill at my passionate wellhead, growl a satisfaction, and release. Partner, who are you? Not rare water to feverish thirst, man, but other river to this strong current. Not fear's subjugator, dude, but my pleasure-brother, shotgun on the wild ride to our twinned peaks. Though fear once brought me, naked, to manboys content to use my body like a hand, though I've met some who gained consent by ill, I still thrill: I come from Orphic depths, from the thousand and one nights I have spent sounding oh, my god.

Therapists, you've been white almost every time. Once, a Desi counsellor broke down in our first and only discussion, blurting her friends' racism. *A Question of Power*, the most understanding female authority I had. The sorrow for which I sought relief, they called miscegenation. I wondered what I did wrong, what I should feel, what needs must I be gagging under my social transgressions. I still battle isolation, working to undo lessons my nerves learned from white supremacy, from behavioural paradigms counsellors had hammered into their masters' degrees. I've hauled my soft, forced orifices into office after office. Wide-eyed counsellors were, by my stories of racial unkindness, always shaken, as I was by your easy application of "universal" palliatives to a psyche trapped in polite hellscapes of multicultural mythologies and media tyrannies that your therapies couldn't validate. I've been a pill, not able to chill. My pleasure sought itself in talking endlessly to weigh how often, how innocently, I suffered in your country. Immigrant, your textbooks said, my mother's story appearing in none of them. Troubled, first-generation immigrant you'd help adjust. To what, reports of Black women's desirability metrics on dating apps? To liberal white folks' chokehold on professional virtue? To you? Intimacies only ever remembered my deepest sense of shame: how hard it is, for you, to sit with the true sorrow of shit sandwich stories. Now movements have opened you to Black Lives; maybe you'll refer to me like I referred to Head. But I still can't bend my head around mental health that doesn't humble its assimilative assumptions. When I saw dreamcatchers on this pale woman's wall, I almost turned around. I've learned not to unbosom myself to exoticizing spiritualists. But her eagle feather is carried as   .
Transformatively, Euroculture's trespass now becomes a reference point. We say colonialism. We say intergenerational. Sitting in her room, we look at the gaslight, listen to my body. She urges me to breathe and feel my joy. It's not some country's request to mute raw truths. There's a peace at my core I can someday share, she says. She looks right in my eyes. I believe her.

Little kids believe when you tell them a creator breathed all living things into life. They can't tell live from mechanical, live from simply existing. Neither can I. I remember vividly when stones and I got to be friends; their secret lives of mineral pressures and geological chance were dramas of being, manifested in their shapes. Just the existence of pleasure was miraculous—its overwhelming schism of self into delighted body and delighted mind. Disciplined not by our feeling, but by others' seeing, we were informed of the how and why of things, like "shoulds" and rules: God was untouchable but real, wise Father of all, seer of unavowed ulterior motives. His extraterrestrial eyes were as given as the salutations alders waved. The phenomenality of us posed a natural question my relatives answered with belief: Good God, rivers don't have family! Wildflowers have no wills! Told to believe in invisible afterworlds, but to pooh-pooh fairy story; told He was forest's author, but that forest animals were lesser species; told I was His child, but shown only white children were little angels, I learned to discount both devotee and "pagan." What I think became what's good enough. Knowing that I am, and that I am Creating, drops in and out of poetic fashion. Duncan's coven and Snyder's enthusiasts colonized the diviners' quadrangles; Atwood white-womanned myth; abuse-spitting tricksters keep reckoning what's up. Poets who English forget they restore what Christian literalists dislimbed: a philosophy of observation, the seer's nature, reason from animal fright. Poem, Soul's ghetto. Hey hey hey, say all the poems Englished not by *un*believers but by the never-believed, this language so bully. This English erase it creating! I asked about the authority of Jerusalem's God, and who got to transmit Deity's declensions. So much depends on some human translation! From Goddish to Hebrew to English—who wrote the supernatural invisible? It was always this guy, these men, to whom He revealed His verses. Meanwhile, the eyes in my head interacted with refractions of Light, and awareness itself lived my nerves. Invite God into your heart, Grandmère commanded, be saved. I wanted to tell her there is no "in" there. The miracle is a tongue's invisible address, and ourselves, shapes breathing our g–dness.

On Thursday, I ingested fifteen healthy tablespoons of sugar hidden within my breakfast protein shake. I'm full of fructose, the sugar as addictive as coke. My orange juice is laced with lethal taste, my salad dressing's made with maltose. I'm trying to weigh my sandwiches: how harmful this challah? how bad this brioche? Best believe that white bread's a killer. Can your crackers remain on the shelf beyond all expiry date? Will those buns survive into eternity? For, at the least, so long as my brain and heart have need for feed, I'll stuff my face. But I'm built hangry, made by nature to sugar-binge on roots and berries, to eat as if I'll winter on my fat. A chocolate torte with glazed lingonberry shouts, "live a little!" to my DNA. Corn syrup is the devil these days—in ketchup, in SpaghettiOs, yoghurt, frozen foods, Light Miracle Whip, cereal bars, Ritz, chips, NyQuil, relish, chocolate milk, and hard candy—now every body can be a diabetic! I don't miss those days of youth when fear of fat had me puking in bathrooms of burger restaurants. My intention couldn't ever stop my appetite; so much holding back only forced my need. I tallied grams of fat psychotically until bad dates rearranged my self-loathing. I moved on to score hits of humiliative reinforcement from boyfriends instead. Give-myself-a-break or pretty-much-let-myself-go? I can't tell maintenance from micromanagement, so I either swear off restraint or get all turbo-controlled. Now they've got apps that refuse to generate those tables that predict your weight loss if you haven't munched enough kilogram calories—smart—that's to keep people like young me off the #ana feeds. Now I just recognize my cycles: I went through a sugar-free hormone-free vegan motion before, that time I hoped to save my womb. And hmm, this week I measure out my life with tablespoons. What gives? This time, this poem's where I exert control. I'll eat to finish this project, to appease what forgot, if it ever knew, what fullness is, the meaning of contentment.

No, Christian, it does/not matter that you shamelessly provoke. It does/ not matter that you boast that single-handedly you changed the x = y of poetry / you never claim single-handedness, you are always attributing a lineage to the form your prowess takes. It might/not, tomorrow, matter that at parties you spout mildly alt-right small talk. To me those strategies are nothing novel, nothing strange; they are but predictable ripostes to the risings of a formerly oppressed lineage. When we meet, our geek dates are brief and not private, but they are always, foremost, about poetry. We admire what the Oulipians did, the constraints they foisted upon themselves—vive Queneau's hundred thousand billion sonnets! We have to admire their translations too. *La Disparition* de la lettre et d'Anton Voyl was Herculean, a user's manual for keeners of the lipogram. Are we born to our desires to best what's done before? I think a certain cutthroat best's quite Western, and I'm a L'Abbé, with forefathers to anxiously succeed. Vowel-slower, crystallographer, Asperger rubber-shoulder, you're a brother who hangs with racist muthas. You've lain with such mangy, gross ideologues, I hesitate, Christian, to distinguish the eunoia from the body that encoded it. But, for posterity, I do. You will not win any prize for understanding or compassion; you might teach an anti-representational norm. You still might in meatspace be insisting, for the petty pleasure of it, that the corporeal doesn't matter and white privilege is a myth. We see you. And yet your triumphant grappling with language is/not made more or less breathtaking by your interpersonal antipathy. For you, composition isn't about expressing authentic anything—politic, perhaps, given capital's your true love. I still hat tip your mannerist workmanship. You're a master builder; my inner architect is moved. I bow to such crystalline line design within such strenuous challenge. My verse won't best *Eunoia*; nor does it wish to. Bro, my procedural line is/not indebted to you. I name your influence, despite the way your snark has justly tanked your currency. I just hope to hell posterity can understand and our heirs can forgive me.

If I believe his malarkey, I am his dear love and his actions were but the chance, miscalculated advance of lust. Almost two years post-violation, I still might flip open my computer and find, waiting for me, a stunner. This hapless bastard's creep game's been unfathomable: I receive pleading emails, with subject lines like "you have to let it go," "forgive me, sweet love," or "though technically you might consider this harassment..." Yes, I wrote him in clear words to never approach me. Yes, on my Instagram and Twitter feeds, he's blocked. I unfriended him and his followers within days following the crime. Still, I gather evidence: I don't block my inboxes; I filter. That I *was* bullied, each email declares inadvertently, that far from accidental intrusion did I suffer. His are the actions of one who won't listen, who smiles while waiting for protest to temper, who nods while on his deaf ears fall words he of course understands, but that he'll blow off. He's thoroughly appalled at the idea that his conduct bore intent. What happened was rape, he'll admit to that technical definition, but not to having intended harm—and will ignore the agential message of my stone unresponsiveness (that followed the ask to quit his phone calls, his texts, his friend requests) to assert and assert that assault is not his policy. He gets that harassment's another crime, technically, but he wants to save our relationship. Or is he just a coward who knows how the system works? Online and at my doorstep and at the university office, his exhortations arrive in number, each detailing the hours of that bad date in his journalistic detail. He's building a plot I'd need to refute if I ever took a stand. His remorse is so hugely politic that he shaped it into an article the *Globe* ran, on how men struggle with rape culture (oh, he sent that link, I couldn't read it). Instead of breaking down, I sat down with Jónína; we shared stories of white male appropriators. In this memo I witness my calm. Like the FBI guy, Comey, I collect my memory to the best of my documenting, anticipating a time when I might be charged to publicize a powerful man's insecure emails. The disinformation goes into a folder. The Cloud is witness to who has lived, and who has lived without answering for, a crime.

Winsome sister! Self-taught looker-out for number one! How did you become so sure the world would canopy you? How did the world not disencumber you of such expectations, but instead, after making the outward show of indifference to young girls' desirings, reconsidered and laid great abundances decorously at your feet? You never felt imperfect for wanting what you wanted—hindered, maybe, challenged, sure, but you never disapproved your own desire. Glam opera promised the stage you wished for, but the soprano in you wanted stage *and* contemporary vernacular, silver and the silver lining. You wished to grant voice and embodiment to others' characters, sure that the talent dwelling in your one little finger could translate into form any dramatists' text. Our faith in talent-over-coming-odds was youthful virtue we'd each lose, and rally, again and again. You moved to Toronto, learned by playing to the casting directors, learned much about the markets for talent and for "commercial" complexions. Sunrise, sunset, when did she grow to be so baller? Climb every mountain, forge every possible relationship with streaming content makers. Simple Simon met an executive producer going to the playwrights' festival. Beautiful sister, to thrive as actress meant submitting to their gazing. Shakespeare's women were teenage boys, but will they cast a modern brown Ophelia? "Wholesome," "buxom," "fresh-faced": quiet codes for blushy skin that you hoped your agent would ignore, but agents don't take on "causes" that cost their outfit money. On Obsidian's platform you apprenticed, organizing productions that proved Black clout. Your friends denied their whiteness ever played a part. You chose to cruise beyond Ontario, mixed with officers, earned good coin as diva six nights a week. On international waters, a Canadian passport meant you got respected as "brunette." Something mutual was possible out there, beyond borders: you found love right where your mien was taken for trophyesque. Now you play the romantic lead that you always could have brought to screen: married to the handsome captain, living on the Riviera, yummy mummy jetsetter. You stayed true to something queenly that allowed you to have nice things. I marvel at your unsentimental performance of a Kitchener kid's chutzpah—I'm endlessly learning from you, sister, how much deserving might be within my control.

Go into the forest, sit under the Amazon canopy. Rain falls. Above, the leafy ceibos' layered crowns echo. Rain hits the flying moss, thumps on woody understorey. Do trees have their own songs? Like birders intimate with species' identifiable *chick-ker-lee!*, dendrologists can suss the trees' IDs from sonic data, says Haskell. Different shapes of leaf produce different whispers or thwacks; different branchy frameworks sway trees' resonatings. "Go out, pour attention willingly into ears, and learn to harvest sound." Repeat your attention, show the forest the sensibility you show lovers. With time, soon each tree rings to patient listeners its pithy, sweet song. Relationally, forests grow. Such a thing as "individual" is foreign to this nature; sovereignty is only meaningful to the system entire: what then, is sovereign in our internetworked frack? Gagliano has faced the scorn of colleagues for listening to *zea mays*, to the corn plant's growing baby roots. Those loud clicks, "acoustic emissions," are incidental, say stalwarts, they're just a mechanical result of plant bubbles cracking in their tissue. But Gagliano suspects the sound-spikes are like talk. She keeps heeding the call of green things, avowing that they purr with sensible purpose, trusting that her ecologist skill may in time divulge the obscenities and graces of plant discourse. Water etches sound into biome; is it only fauna that hears? Kind-listening-kind, possible yet feared, without ears, the outside hears our eartheathearth. A balsam fir zings and tinks as chickadees raze cones of their purple scales; its verdure converses with vapour. An olive's branch extends over human military detonations, breathing dust and curling into itself. The scientist will keep, while hearing trash-talk, measuring the unheard-of "auditory" knack of green peas: through desiccated soil, they foray toward water held in pipes, answering the sound of moving water without ever tasting its moisture. Vibes. Plants. Sounding the nervous quiet of us, bodies, phytosentient. O render xylem phonetics, their phlo)(   )(   )(em.

127

I'm staring at Shakespeare's poem. Blocked. Carnage because Black was
not counted fairly. Torn into faithless weather because literature assured
Black bodies bore no right to beauty's name, because until now is Black's
traumatology streaming in successive waves. The critics never unpack the
intestinal douleur of one's own beauty slandered with a bastard shame.
Informed since I could read by the monarchy's hand on the throat of
English, I've put on an enunciative face, trusting the figure of speech's
power to fair the ink of English thinking. The foreign anguish, language!
With art's facelessness I borrowed legit face; with my sweet syntax, a
beauty that they couldn't disown. Shame on who? Shame on who? I'm
literally bowed over the keyboard of my computer. Sometimes you see
yourself profaned. Sometimes you're profaned—nothing unusual—by the
archives you're working in. Why feel disgraced in two thousand seven-
teen? Le professeur francophone que j'ai rencontré on Bumble blanks at
my imaginary stresses: okay, your poems are about race, but we don't have
to think in black and white over dinner, do we? Somebody doesn't. This
situation suits some bodies just fine, and they will date me, if I don't bring
work home. I'm churning through Shakespeare's sonnet, contemplating
easier occupations. My children, who were not born into fairness, who no
beauty ever lacked, who never happened at all, read this grudging cre-
ation over my shoulder. They are with me always, as I fail at ease. They
don't exist, as I cleave to my poetry like a significant other who never asks
anything of me, who isn't hurt by my inability to lighten up. Nothing's
coming, just a gust of weather, a failure to work through a sonnet's hatred.
Slavery's tongue is in my head, kissing me, saying smile, smile, beauty
shouldn't look so hard.

How often, Dad, when we dreamed, was the dream house mentioned? You imagined a rustic plot, exposed beams, a huge studio out back. A piece of land for clay and fire's meeting. Studio-pottery-as-return-to-the-land: Steele did it at Nanoose Bay; Laffin and Ngan established wood kiln workshops on Hornby; a hippie team with potter Lari Robson sought and found their craftsman work hideouts on a hill above Booth Bay. Those West Coasters wet their fingers in salt water while you, Northern Ontario kid, lugged your kin to Calgary, to cast with Askey and Ungstad, to throw wetware with Gord Robertson at Ceramic Arts. Your communal enclave of potters was a different whack at modernist *mingei*, commercialism and craft confounded, a business-minded Orientalist folk movement. Did you make those jars, or could they be Katie Ohe's? The unknown craftsman ideal might work for humble village potters of Japan, but in commercial markets, your mark is your aesthetic take on Leach's brand, named and circulated. The inward, forceful touch of your hand, its weighted, skilled pressure, left impressions— your pots' forms like performances of workmanship, each an ethos of harmony, of function (how well does that handmade pitcher pour?) balancing individual expression. Stoneware napkin rings, teapots with cane handles, wood-fired soup bowls, decanter sets, mugs by the hundreds, bottles, jugs: your shapings of extracted land, in folk tradition borrowed by avant-gardists and Black Mountain ceramicists, were work. You lived the philosophy, threw as though art worlds rewarded character, fine galleries' patronage would heighten our state and situation, and sweat equity in handcraft would build that house. That dream, utopian fabrication, forged me. I chose inkjet and paper as rough materials; in workshops, practiced forms. By touch my fingers now know how to translate, to make, my rawness into a thing, presentable, wedged out of capitalist making. I'm living the dream on the Island, in Harewood, in the middle of nowhere, blessed, I guess, to chase such singular surviving. Meanwhile, hobbyist potters step into your space just to sit with authentic mastery. Japan jacked Korean skills; did Shoji Hamada live appropriately? Lari died in two thousand twelve. Robin Hopper's garden lives on. For this poem, an internet search of your early work found just two things. A casserole on Calgary Craigslist. And a late mid-century decanter. This vintage guy in Lantzville, whose teak lamps decorate my bedroom, has it. He balked at a discount, even though I said I was your kid.

The expensive rock on her finger comes from the Republic of Congo. The Central African Republic is split into factions; wars separate people from shelter and medicines. The lust for diamonds fuels extraction, and fights over who will control extraction fuel mistrust. Angola's government is perjured, murderous, bloody, full of blame, savage. Extreme brutality in the diamond fields. Zimbabwe's cruelty to unofficial miners is documented, but who can control Mugabe? Sly traders enjoy diamond-fed chaos. But blood violence, boring. Brutality, despicable yet so overexposed. A machete cuts straight past reason; hunters never need reason; domination gives no reason. For so long, here at home, I have asked perpetrators to give reasons, to say why they hate dialogue, as if reason forces another to swallow dissent. There's a band of interaction, purposeful and respectful, like a dimension one can enter or miss, a frequency of kindness that the lucky take for granted. Some girls get a diamond from their dad. Some diamonds are given in pursuit and some diamonds signal possession; some women have diamond chokers; some have rings. Diamonds are a girl's best insurance in unequal power situations. There's a violent extreme? There's a virginal bliss, brilliant, sparkling, cut. A ribbon. Who wants their fiancée's precious commodity to prove depraved? North of Yellowknife, Blusson and Fipke found diamondiferous kimberlite pipes. Before long, a mine was joyfully proposed, and Canada became ethical diamond leader. The stones are marked with laser logos of ethicalness so the world well knows from whom to buy. They built Diavik, an open mine on a lake floor. The nation of Attawapiskat weathers hardsells to marry DeBeers. "For ethically conscious consumers, these diamonds are the squeaky-clean fave," insists the luxury trade article. Canada's got no wars worth mentioning, so it's safe to say these diamonds are hella conflict-free.

My muse, made by distress, has never met my eye. His glances return only
the indifference that struggle mistakes for strength. Isn't a poet's muse an
emotional construction, an ideal devised by fear of more redblooded con-
tact? The Romans got theirs from Delphi—practice, song, and memory,
or else soundings of waters, air, and voice—wondered as beautiful women.
The ancients knew that poetry moves through a body as resonance, as har-
monies: the hero's brave accomplishments, a girl's rare decorum, the scent
of loosestrife and hyacinth, are but subjects to the wind in the poet-lyre.
The muse ennobles the hack: without Euterpe, song is mere howling; sans
Melpomene, heroes' heads roll without grace. What vibes temper a versify-
ing personality? That's the question disarmed by imagining skills as god-
desses, genres as goddesses. We're aiming toward ideals, always—maybe
Hesiod tried to fill a youthful-nymph-shaped hole in his unconscious;
maybe Homer and Herodotus sheepishly beseeched Calliope and Clio in
the very voice Humbert Humbert used to invoke the seraphic nakedness
of his nymphette. All wisdom and knowledge personified as sublime sis-
ters is heroine-craft I'm down for—wherever delight and thankfulness for
feminine authority are its root. Sappho's fragmented breath, that comes
down to us from Mytilene, made her mistress of the Greeks—I love to
hear her poems speak, enthused Plato, who hyped her as the tenth muse.
But Sappho dug women, and allured when invoking the Muses, drop-
ping wows on their hair. Flattering femme muses isn't my schtick: I'm no
Athenian, no forefather inflamed by virgin/whore pleiades, no modern
painter goddessing young ladies after gallery galas. In fact, I never saw a
goddess for whom I'd go to my knees. I'm my own mistress. But when I
sigh, a perfect knowledge hears me, surely? I invoke the perfect listener,
who reads my expressions without error, who gets my ninja warrior allu-
sions—omg, some idealized blend of dad and boyfriend—with whom my
throbbing psyche craves communion . . . Everything I seek is inside myself
—love, understanding, security—say relationship experts. So, anybody in
there? Listener, hello? Something bodied listens, eyes down, awaiting the
hard cuff of false compare.

131

The Boulevard Club must have stifled a shudder when my mom rang to inquire about memberships. Young Guyanese newcomer hadn't thought about how courts are segregated by those whose bequeathed equities proudly make them "exclusive." At Crawford and Queen, the public hard-surface courts at lowly Trinity Bellwoods didn't wear only whites; her groundstroke forehand powered straight to my dear dad's doting heart. Meanwhile, apartheid South Africa was inviting only the fairest and most PR-friendly competitors to its tournaments. A jewel of Wirrayaraay, they'd let in. To Evonne Goolagong they promised fair treatment, though some say that she shouldn't have agreed to be an honorary white while they denied Arthur Ashe. You faced shame-drills at the corner of Compton and Atlantic, your father testing the power of shame to make you lose your cognitive edge. Like Tiger Woods, you ascended into aristocracy's recreational spheres, where country clubbers game. Rankine's already written a Serena who dares to be so bold as to call out negrophobic umps, while a rival's right to blonde privilege she'll shrewdly let pass. Mine is the Redditor-marrying Serena, living the fantasy more blondes understand. Trophy babe. Signature fashionista hanging with Wintour. Snotty, false friends must swear a thousand allegiances to you, crowned earner. Supermom-to-be, your attractiveness to the sponsorship industry is smoking hot. Companies with your face on their storytelling brand themselves mother-of-all-stamina, conqueress-while-Black. I'm driven to witness: I want to bear the way you do, trusting my Black performance will be assessed fair, that this best linesmanship will meet literary judgment in its place. I want nothing to do with art's false modesty. I want to hold court where Black won't save me. I want the physicality of my deeds, the demand of the excellence. Without a brown girl's desire to play tennis, I wouldn't be here, so manifest of what I think, my game proceeds.

Little chubby fingers, solemn eyes, I love you! Matante is my most distinguished title; you are the specialest baby! Christmas evening, your mom went for a walk—she never goes walking at night—an anomaly that hinted at your ultra-imminent forthcoming. Everyone was at home (it was Christmas): I was home from mid-Island; Jordan didn't have to work; super serendipitously, even Grandmère was blessing us with a quick and loving visit. Your mom and dad returned to our house from their airbnb in the wee hours, looking wide-awake, timing the already pretty regular contractions on a scratch pad. We all got up. Four in the morning, your mom pain-managed through well-honed Hypnobaby birth techniques. The morning sun rose as Dad filled the Aquaborn, overtaxing the basement water heater, so that we became like pioneers in movies, carrying pots heavy with boiling water downstairs. The doula arrived shortly and cheerfully checked your mom's dilation. Soon your father was breath-steadying your mother, who squatted in the half-full pool, as we all stared and breathed. I had your sister up in my arms, holding her as we took in the event. She munched on a sprouted wheat muffin-half, with chocolate chips and peanut butter, as, glorious, you slid into the sober world. Littlest us! Smallest homegirl, Giselle! Now your two mourning eyes burn their overcome into this memory, your face contorted with knowledge: Matante visited you on the ship, six months later. Squiggly wiggle, little beebee, you were a squirmer! The bathroom on the ship was tiny. Changing your wet diaper was a test of manoeuvring. The floor was marble. Since then, I mourn your first knowing, dropped from the wet, the floor was marble—I grabbed, your slick legs, slipped, and smack. Skull, hit. The baby. Picked up in. An instant, you, howling like innocence, violenced. Your mommy appeared. Vomit. Your father summoned down from the bridge. They couldn't tell, Giselle, if your crown was cracked; apparently babies' craniums are soft by design. The terrible swell left in three weeks; the black mark on Matante's id faded. Giselle, your mother instantly forgave me; eventually your father cracked jokes. Little toughy, I saw you, coated in a film of pallid vernix, slip into hands. Now you fall into Matante's lap, commanding me to read *Five Little Monkeys*.

This bespoke thinking is written without bias. I disconnected my heart—that makes my head in charge. From the vantage point of the fact gatherer, from the angle of neutral observer, detached from feels, I articulate privately-funded research into the power to publicly find information. Wikipedia gives my friend and me license to create an entry on Fred Moten, but not to ensure its longevity; at least thirty-two thousand editors can contribute to my remedial education on celebrity butts' cleavage (aka posterior rugae). The slippery encyclopedia lives as freely as computer literacy does, as Westernly as tech anarchist first principles soon harden into masculine structures. Believe me, says the format, but not too much. My students are told: verifiability, not truth. You'll get the cruel eye from the academic establishment if you make reference to Wikipedia's take on democracy in your next political science editorial. After English, the Cebuano language boasts the most articles, due to Sverker Johansson's Isjbot, says the internet. Sixty thousand page requests per second, says one page; four thousand, says another. Freshmen editors feel more chummy with insider culture than females, says the Wikimedia Foundation, on the Wikipedia item informing us about Wikipedia. In twenty fourteen, the Foundation promised to increase their outreach to chicks, but it's years since, and the girl-to-dude ratio is almost seven-fold, still, for the guys. I tell you this because information is sourced, and poetry is information. My heart isn't hyperlinkable, so relax. There's a digital humanities bro or seven on the geek end of William's Wikipedia entry, doubter, but the references are even more manly, so it's a fact: the playwright existed and is the greatest writer who ever lived, insist many people who never read him, and some who have. These overwritings of bardic legacy are Wikipedia harvests, sometimes; sometimes this work condenses peer-reviewed consensus. Sometimes I let my heart take a back seat to head; sometimes, its guard is for the common good. I futz with canonic texts like a lit librarian demonstrating how easy it is to abuse Wikipedia; with rigour I insert my facts into Project Gutenberg's "free, plain, vanilla" document. Will Wikipediocracy vet me? Watchdogs tussle over Wikipedia's flaws; Breitbart calls the information behemoth left-wing. Conservapedia, Infogalactic, and Britannica: these are the options. A search for articles that *mention* Wikipedia is a shitshow. The engine thinks you want Wikipedia articles about all the things. I just want to query what is informed.

Leanne Simpson throws a stone into the water of our shared lives. My confessional mode, that helps middle-class individualists share their neuroses, isn't adequate for minding the many self-awarenesses Simpson models on Michi Saagiig Nishnaabeg territory. Her miigwech to so many begins, rather than ends, her work. An opening, into the family-wound I feel in my self. On Turtle Island, this self—can I forfeit its ego, its heart so othered it clings to "mine"? Though she writes in English, Turtle Island stories through Betasamosake Simpson's story. I'm comforted and stilled, learning about the Indigenous insides I am without. When I listen, my root listens, wondering not only where I am, but who else is alive here. Listening to concept of dibaajimowinan, wondering how settlers write responsibly in English. O, grandmotherskin! My body's life force, creative force, inextinguishable! My matriarchs, taught by convent schools, what is left of us, so Canadianned, here? Simpson's books, an inside shared, where I learn a desubjugation that my unsure identity likens. This   opening, not written for me. I was not born under that bond. But when I am with Simpson, I am in a safer address, T-Dot in Nishinaabemowin, downtown Peterborough as restated, unmuted Nogojiwanong. That safety, where the healthy beauty of Nishinaabeg thought flowers, resists the colonialist take, talks with Haudenosaunee. I'm unsure how to carry my settler heritage, as I pen an unwhiteness, out myself as generation of forced intercourse, unpassing-half-breed of land and territorial abuse. Born on Turtle Island, how should I embody nation? Like my ex-friend who practiced yoga competitively, I'm absurd, elbowing shared story into an egoic form. I mean to yoga Betasamosake Simpson, where I am, immersed in her telling. She shows me o a on ei a , o ue ou , u i i a e yu i i o ee u , o i i a ea . Maybe that's us, and we haven't yet a e e i that will shut our mouths to a e u . I swallow story that's older than church, older than any subject borne of enlightenment, than any school teaching my angst's descent from Hamlet's. Through bodies, her page says. My motherhood, my wo/manhood, decodes survival as resistance. E ii aa i , e practice, teaching me an innership not for me to confess.

When I'm stoned, I can't versify. Euphoria opens the channels to raw archives in the body, the words rush past the psyche's will to stay grounded, and I willywaw onto the blank page. For hours, I can sit and write squalls of inchoate nerve burp, blurts of moral predictability, gushes of interplanetary transmission. Ugh, am I that vapid the next day? Yes, the devastating brilliance I owe to tetrahydrocannabinol is as wicked fresh as the word *devastating* modifying the word *brilliance*. But the making's the thing when I add a bit of Durban Poison; with kush, working feels like inputting holy genius waves into the conscious universe. When I'm lit, possibility is large and spacious. No quarter ounce removes all the ouch, but I feel safe to unhide my own hidden columns and believe in the power of sincerity. Shame follows me into professional circles, sort of. I can't mother myself into straight edge morality; straight guys who only drink disapprove; even some alcoholic poets judge. So what, say friends, you're in B.C. In my hood, Harewood, fentanyl's killing off teen partiers; Kelowna was a cocaine hotspot, where students would dance up to me, shining, to confess they'd swallowed MDMA. Don't all writers down antidepressants, or else type their rehab fiction, or memoir about giving head for smack or about addictions to eating? I missed alcohol's attraction; I didn't ever do a bump. But when I dance in dank's augmented headspace, every movement worships the moment, worships existence. Popping gesture to syncopated beat, I metamorphose music. The reverb of being ricochets in my wrist roll, hard-angled thrash, boogaloo, or tetris. I mash freestyle vogue femme with lyrical hip hop, needing no writing to translate this soul of mine; in the syntax of motion, I carve a kinetic poem into night sky. A blunt is a bridge between psychological and vegetal, between money-making and green leaves, between drives toward sun or dark. In the yard, I grind a nug, roll a fattie, light, and draw green breaths. The spruce and cedar, who watch over the grass, welcome me back to animality. La, says my guitar. The knives glint in the kitchen drawer. A law criminalizes me now, but soon, pharmaceutical companies will sell dime bags. I go into the office to sit and squamish, thinking one day I'll rewrite this brilliantly.

A fifteen-hundred-and-fifty-square-foot bungalow in Kitchener, back then, was gettable, with Dad at the print shop, commuting before dawn, plus Mom's nine-to-five admin gig at the university. They worked four years to erase the bankruptcy, building a downpayment from stone broke. Unimaginable, now—that recouping, the workability of real-estate goals sans wealthy uncle willing you hundred-thousands. I worked at Swiss Chalet, clearing three measly bucks an hour, in high school, and who knows how many gigs in undergrad, until my middle-class identity got shocked in Jakarta. There, the house my uncle's family (otherwise from Niagara Falls) had looked very much like a two-storey on Glenholme Ave., except surrounded by razor wire. It was, by Western standards, fairly humble, but for nail-spiked walls, iron-grilled windows, and the fellow with the firearm, sullenly fixed in the stall at the entrance to the gated suburb. A driver often slept in the company vehicle overnight, in the driveway, if they'd kept him late. A docile maid tiptoed, her hands full with washing and my aunt's pills. The air-conditioned mall had a Macy's and a KFC. It was built for a class of Indonesians who routinely page their waiting chauffeurs after hard days of shopping. There's still a KFC at Fraser and Broadway, in once-grittier Mount Pleasant, its two-fifty-chicken-Tuesdays now eschewed by hipster power vegans whose money drives gentrification. Humbler hoping millennials reckon it's not grandad's economy anymore: that apartment in Strathcona rents for four times what boomers' monthly payments were on mortgages. Pass judgment on the "flood" of foreign wealth, on "ultra-rich Asians" buying up Chinatown and Shaughnessy, but the real estate horrorshow is neoliberalism's wake, the crank of income inequality ratcheted by the point-one-percent. Mansion or crack house? asks the website, showing shacks going for tons more than a million. Van's ghetto landlords mention discounts for friends with benefits. People's leases are paper-thin; dwellers hold off that renoviction with nothing more than a phrase. Twenty-somethings would have to not eat seventeen thousand avocado toasts, however, to make a bid on an Oakridge condo. So. Build a wall, shouts the memory of an American manufacturing heyday. A humble home in Vancouver—laser motion detectors, or

137

nylon and velcro? Kidlets with master's degrees and three side hustles are unlanded non-immigrants with no expectations; East Van household-ers can't get over their stratosphere. Me, I found a three-bedroom with a yard, only two hundred and ten minutes from Kits, and two thousand miles from my blood.

Go until you throw up, go blind, chafe, or collapse, says an ethos. Overachiever, what does this ultramarathon justify? You want discriminate eyes to measure what they behold, and see not only what isms they are told to see, but to cheer the odyssey of unknowing what beauty is, to share the weight lifted by endurance literatures, literatures of tenacity. If they're still with us at this point, the forebears tisk, they're already keeners. They say willpower is a myth, that obeying or trying to fake yourself is about control. This procedure sports in part by overthinking, in part by playing onomatopoeically, over and over, like some being anchored in a straightjacket, some being anchored in a body, who achieves no more than letting go. Do ultramarathoners run like this, ride waves of hurry, waves of urgency, on legs restless for release? Who could thrive by castigating themselves into such unforced doggedness? How do keeners know where to exercise their joules? A pledged commitment of my heart: it's what I've searched for, writing this. If you should think I knew my heart's goal, think again: this heart hasn't ever been allowed to openly control which direction my push propels. This art doesn't know; it does. The-wide-eyed-world-meets-the-common-despot, also known as a-sucker-is-born-every-minute, is a basic energy. It compels poets, who, seeing the ordinariness of anguish, become daily about their sweat. Compulsion is not discipline; I'm no marathoner for putting years of effort into calming down. Try, try, again until you throw up, break down, see spots, says scarcity. Follow your bliss, hard, until you faceplant, insists slapstick. They say running for five minutes, every day, might add three years to your life. If I set my heart on a final distance, maybe I'll rush, and stop once I've crossed a line. Or, I could care less about destinations, and devote myself to this fitness. I've talked in circles, steeplechasing a hundred and thirty-seven times, over hurdles I set myself, to get nowhere objective—so far. But it adds up. I can almost see my core, transformed by so much fear burned off.

139

White skin supremacy loves to swear on spit tests that social hierarchies are made of genetic truths. I don't believe whiteness is categorical, though I know someone who calls herself white reinforces that hallucination. She might think white means European. She might be an executive, steering race like an untutored youth drives her daddy's car, unlearned at considering the world's false science or aggression's subtleties, thus vainly thinking that she thinks open-mindedly about rungs. Although she knows her gran's mentality, those days are past, she tells herself. The best simply rise to the top; she credits her own good family values and hard work when she's on speaking tours. When eugenicists rouse protest, she wants to hear "both sides." The success of certain genes, to her, is a simple truth correctness suppresses; it's sad for the weak, but what else can we derive in the face of Western heritage's authority? Others ask twenty-three-and-me to establish their Indigeneity. It's unjust to use blood quantum to undo where you're from; it's how governments say you're not Status Indian, teach Tallbear and âpihtawikosisân. Meanwhile, a Willowdale doctor's kid's apologetics are leveraged with DNA swab results. Half-brown, half-white, is how I identified, back when I saw that seeming white inspired trust, and that genetic background complications overcomplicated Canadian conversations. But melding my own mulatto and Baloch mélange into convenient Guyanese was a strategy, a story told by British educators, meant for another coloniality. I've got some Brit in the woodpile, so "technically" I'm more than fifty percent European. I tried to share that claim with mates, and learned Canadian as a euphemism for purity. Fathers, if we're so ultimate, somebody explain to me how my superior white phenotype is so utterly flattened by a random drop of beige?

O! Don't call me bystander! Don't make me struggle to justify my silence before the wrongs that the golf-shirted confederacy do. Your unkind witness lays a doily upon my heart; you wound me. I'm not a white-right hick, not violent. Those yokels are brutes; their whiteness has nothing of my enlightened schooling. You confuse their abuse of power with my power, and slay me with ungracious evaluation. I buy Inuit art; don't tell me that's not enough. My love is invested elsewhere; I banish brutes from consciousness; my sight allows all my dear heart can take. For bearing ill will toward ugliness just stokes angers; I protect my shine from anxiety. When a friend's aside shows a little hate, you need to just ignore it, rather than open up wounds with accusation. Why ruin a nice evening, when they might be going through something tough at work, when they're human family otherwise? Oppression is a big word; anyone would get defensive at being called tyrannical. I need to bide my time; I need to let stews simmer; I need to excuse myself from this seat at the table. I want a home rosy with love; I want to be sure my little girl knows her pretty looks aren't shameful. I've been open-minded; I don't want enemies, and yet, here you are, throwing forefathers' old missteps in my face. Maybe it's your hard feeling that turns family into foes. Making everything about what white boogeyman do is ugliness; it's reverse-painting all white people. I am overwhelmed right now; how dare you suggest that the irreparable injuries liberal democracy has met do not scorch my soul! I am able-bodied too, do you then say I oppress the handicapped? Really, Sonnet, I am nearly suicidal watching the news. If I'm so bad, kill me outright for my white-witchy looks, and rid the savage planet of my needless compassion.

Be wise as you scroll; don't read the comments. Regular hatreds, habitual cruelties gather under reports of a teen shot by a farmer, citing property. Comments some body, feeling tongue-tied and impatient with "correctness," writes to show the nation's conscience. So much disdain aggregates under articles that sites close comments. Sorrow explodes along bodies' memory-lines when Canadians' words express the table manners of supremacy. "Pity-wanting," proud taxpaying citizens call the calls to fairness. What might teach empathies, councilmen waive: there's better political power-play in hackles raised. Scroll through; don't open yet another video of colloquial anti-Black violence. You must protect yourself, over and over, from too much telling. You must open yourself to things-as-they-are. Nasty women, sick men. People who rationalize when the unfair deaths of brown people happen nearby. No news is good news, for bullies gutting healthcare, for sensitive boos minding their physician's advice. I don't want to know and information is power. Without fam I should despair, but with all the hatesnark I should go mad, and in my madness I might speak ill into the faithcraft of equities. What's news, anyhow? The resistance-killers' words, once spat as they wrestled others into ground, now hang around in screenshots. "Public discourse" is no longer owned by bourgeois old boys whose bad behaviour never made headlines. We scroll. My vagina hardens into a fist when criminal lawyers glibly affirm that some bodies get what they deserve. Some bodies believe in dirty bodies, and want their own cleanness screamed. Like that white guy who raged that the East Indian girl he married had already been violated. He'd meant her to be so innocent. On our date, he shook his fist, to show me: *her cunt! impenetrable! like this!* I asked to be spared the details. He looked me in the eyes, and said he wanted to ram it into her, but was a good guy. I can't hear that, I said, you should go. He stumbled closer, breathing heavily, his proud heart beating to expound, pound, pound us into the Wild West.

Picture clingfilm wrapping the entire Earth. I do not mean like Christo's eleven islands that he wrapped with millions of square feet of pink poly-propylene, or the coast and cliffs of Australia, bundled in synthetic. Or maybe I do. Since the Second World War we've synthesized enough plastic to wrap around the Earth a layer of unrottable polymer. South Philippine coasts are invisible under tons of floating supermarket bags, syringes, hang-ers, cartons, toothpaste tubes, deli gloves, watchstraps, bottles, cheaply made desk supplies, and bejewelled cellphone casings. Decades of plastic clutter our eon's future view; islands of plastic agglomerate; goulashes of marine debris. Tote lids, videotapes, non-reuseable cream containers, gel containers, sandwich bags, dirty dish cloths, yoghurt containers, action figures, tags, unrecycled panelling, and hotel do-not-disturb signs take hundreds of years to fade to molecules. Scientists are going to base geologi-cal observations on human-led changes, as particles of polystyrene, nylon, and polyethylene terephthalate settle into sediments, or as melted plastic globs harden into new "plastiglomerate" stone. Microbeads invade fish tissues, adding exfoliants to many conscientious epicures' healthy feasts —tuna gritty with phthalates; red salmon goosebumped with methacry-late filler. Predictive wits think oceans, by approximately twenty-fifty, will have more plastic weight than fishes. What can dissuade my convenience-foolish heart from single-serving string cheese? White bottle caps live unsullied inside Midway Atoll's dead albatrosses; the little auklets wash up on Vancouver Island's shores. No literal floating masses of landfill, yet, in the gyres of the Pacific. Nurdle soups eddy and gather. Water bottles sell water. Every dram second every thirty thousand sales water. Retch thousand bottles only to million by plastic gulls water. Thus far I count my garbage kitchen, three water bottles cheap to half a trillion. Clear plastic makes me sin sealed. Water, bubble, wrap doesn't pop anymore? We can haz water, packaging.

143

No LOLs voluted into swastikas on my skin. No anchors entwined with my dearest's name, no virtues inside hearts, no blue hearts inscribed with "courage" or "faithful" on my skin. No girls with wounded eyes on my skin, no champagne flutes full of love's cursive lettering, no butterflies with meaningful quotes comparing struggle to hatching out of a chrysalis, no seeds blowing from understated dandelions across my left shoulder. No "seek & you shall totally find it," no mermaids whose tails dissemble into a turbulence of paired doves, no rearing unicorns lifting twisted horns above candytuft rainbows, no "Mother," no parted red lips open for pert cherries on my neck. The tattooed haven't profaned their skin; scarifiers don't defile, either. With ornaments we brand ourselves visual, define naturalness, declare our becoming. No QR codes, no infinity symbols, no "everything happens for a perfect reason," no semi-colon stamp of the recovery tribe, no borrowed "other's" real tribe's design rounds my bicep. No "Believe" in curlicues, no feather-trimmed dream catcher encircling a netmesh of beads, no nautical stars, no "to thine own self be true." No "live, love, laugh," no mystic healing runes, no "dance as though" along my clavicle. No Buddhist lotus, no English rose, no widebrushed om-in-Sanskrit thingy; no blue-eyed stoic wolves. No Jays logo, no Minions, no "carpe diem," no pi or quadratic equation. No Celtic mythic tree root, Celtic pirate lady, or Celtic knot embellishes my chest; no handwritten "that which doesn't kill us makes us stronger" adorns my wrist. Why not imprint any image on my dermis? What nerve I have to print image in indelible ink fronts in this book. Pulped page, forest skin, thinking pigmented. I ink into the ectodermal nervous system; I draw hashtags, trash polka gas mask tableaux, biohazardous material symbols into your hidebody. Into myself, I uncarve exes. I'd have tramp-stamped nichol's pome, maybe. If pomes were letters. Or a line. About how language cubes, kinside, inkside of your body body body.

Look at you, cousin, Canadian as any boxcarful of refugees. From else-where, you showed up with your family, here, in our town. You struggled to catch on to local kindergarten ideas of here, of regular, of the ordinary, as children asked about your accent. Shy little brother, you took time, learned the way some settlers disown their backgrounds because Canada makes Us All Immigrants. Wide-eyed, place-fathered, you discovered playgrounds teach who is in pursuit, and who pursued. Your father thwacked tennis balls and flighty shuttlecocks with our loner dad; your mother behaved Christianly, while she and my mother negotiated lives in this country, raised us children. Who held losers down when sporting chase? Whose cries whooped the game of catch-the-sucker? Who escaped the teacher's busybody care? You were in the same grade as my brother. You learnt to follow the same red and white flag, which flies over befriendings, and over a sense of here's faces. Soon your native pronunciations fizzled. Alien no more, you grew into here's no-problem sporting fan, accentless, discon-tent with social rejects. You, Johnny-come-lately, sitting in our kitchen, complaining about draft picks and foreigners. Your father, ingratiated with local rich folk, trained his son to fraternize. You made the teams while I started fearing athletes' fratty babe-chasing hazes; you were T-shirted and ball-capped into early fraternity. Boy-next-door, youthful family friend, I heard about you all my life—the outstanding catch that you hopped a fence to snag, your cool on the back nines, the toll of semi-pro. But teams' weekend dirty play, I gather from your grandmother, spoiled the game for you. Who's legit to kiss? Not me, I bet. Your kind shows no kneel on-field. A policeman now, you perch in our kitchen, explaining why eight cops have to throw down one Muslim man. You make sergeant, show us a fun video where they taser you while laughing. But *I* was here first. *I* was born here. Of course we shouldn't turn *you* back toward your homeland. But maybe Loku would be alive, maybe Abdi and Coriolan would be, if white boys didn't get so striped into jocular violence?

Tory declares war on you black-masked omnivores. Smiling, he launches "an offensive" on offending raccoons, who make life in Toronto such an ordeal. He describes your paw-hands as pilferers' weaponry, as high-tech lock pickers, to outwit with outsourced "private-sector reinforcements." A cinder block strung with bungee cord across the metal-latched lid is tactically quite enough green bin supplement to deter raccoon foragers, some claim, but crooky critters are a mayor's easy wrong to right. Scofflaws, he christens you. Rustlers, he says, whose rustlers' spirits are woe to humans, whose coonish plots require our "most complicated surveillance." He means to win "the battle" against the meddlesome "raccoon nation" with special anti-animal compost bin technology. "No more free meals," you pesky evil patience tempters, he taunts. Shady characters, venal vermin, backyard bandits: it's better if raccoons don't get lunch from humans' recycling bins, but why deride? Animal deference would corrupt a mayor's authority. "Nation": he's kidding. "Nation," says Betasamosake Simpson, of the deer, reverential. With moose and buffalo nations, Anishinaabeg honour treaties. John's purposeful enmity isn't with the lone raccoon forager, survival scrounger; it's with your pride, your nationhood, with sovereignty, here, "beneath" us. "Defeat," mocks Tory, "is not an option." Scavengers, little beasts, urbanized ferality. Furry friends, sly suspects, dumpster divers. "Smart and hungry," Tory warns, "and determined." In his mouth, you sound like a name said incorrectly. Grandmothers tell old knowledge about your behaviour; storytellers sing a ou y ou o a e o i i ea a ou e oo a ou ea, a y ou i ie i a e i i e a ou ou ai. At Yonge and Church, Twitter says, a raccoon became an angel, rose in one paw, joint in another, sprawled honoree of a viral sidewalk memorial. Maybe in two generations you'll pop the bins' lids, hatch a new skill, build new neural networks. You're cute now, but you live in the shadow of Uber Eats, too intelligent for mayors to straight up badmouth. "Trash pandas" are Toronto's ungovernable "unofficial animal frenemy." Oh, that's a good one, insecure foodies lol over ruthless slurs.

Those lips that spoke love were yours, Mom. Your brown hand first touched me kindly, your maternal kisses were commas, between breaths that Englished the world. You brung forth the sound that said "I am" from the earth of me. These poems are the materialization of my languaging, the shh of your soothing, in derivative forms of mothering's sake. But whispering in the brung-she was an ancestry unworded. You pronounced my neural within, Sonnetted my mindfulness, stated my sound strategies of survival in a "good" English trained into great-grandmother's heart. Aunt Alema, whose diction did or didn't matter in this country, always claimed our women tended to scale asylum walls. You whistled do re mi fa, so? You sang out, in that tongue that Canada called vernacular, a sweet dawning of the Age of Aquarius. You swung me, hips winding, to calypso in the living room. You gently tuned my boom-boom, and taught-up this echo string. With Aunt Sally's harmonies are we togethered, Janet. In the sanitorium, Messessa nourished a little garden of her wit, out in the yard. Shut-up for years, for wailing her child gone missing. Later she was the grandmother you followed out into gardens, her gentle skirts a hiding place for you, her doted-on, mischief-making toddler. Swung low and sung to, sprig of childbirth, watered by her cherishing, now you bounce back like a rubber tree, like a ficus elastica, and I spring from your branches. My sibs have the kink in her hair. To her, we owe your sillywillyness; our flow spills granmudda way. Anita heart, we forward into Mila, Giselle, generations, triumphantly, recalling the way she throated "whatever will be" into dementia's landscape. Love's thud dub my life, saying *steups*, Janet mother you.

This new person is my boyfriend. A soul, just outside the centre of my spinning. My fretful heart hears me say yes, come in to my fretful heart. My heart hears me rebuke logic; its own power scares. Here is a guy who says dailiness, who says Sonnet and touches me. Touched, I am all openings. The within and without of me suffer endearment, the pain of wanting, the oxytocin urging me toward him. Alone, I am unwalled, defenceless, untouched. Maybe he comes to play a game with my body, with raw physicality, and my soul is a referee. Gradually he comes to have meaning. This could be a short burst, a release: he doesn't have to be the one. Who undoes my guard? A new person—his somatic history and fears ding my alarms: can self-protection suspend its disbelief? This man won't kill me, won't grind my single heart into his recreation? My softness meets his exercise of masculinity; I'm still learning how to wind up with a boy. The charge of instinct thrills. But the yes of my body to his simple presence is data in another language. Soul, alive on the outskirts of traumatic perception. Faithful body, observant of slowness and inflection, of threat and passion, I smell a friend. After so many aggravations and rapes, the possibility of respectful commerce between us makes me shy. It's early; all breathmints and divine intercourse, all shining hours of discovery and soapsmells. Something within is being fed by witness. The outsider in me, becalmed. Here are kitchen boogies, morning dog excursions, phone calls at small hours. Panicky feelings don't devastate; they rise through this atmosphere. I could feed them stories of mean men and read a weak ethos into his silences, or ride out my avoidant attachment's insurgence. So far, there's nothing more steadying than breathing.

148

I'm sorry. Interlocutor, event organizer, listener, reader: I wasn't safe. I behaved as if we were longing for the same thing. I talked like my longing for that which only my longing sees was understanding, was common ground. I disrespected relationship. Meaning to call out the disease of colonial amnesia, which feeds on being out of touch, on withholding empathies which would jeopardize the empire, I overstepped. Unaware I was being everything I've judged. I didn't handle it well. You pointed out my selfish take; I became uncertain: my sickly appetite to please has never questioned my reason for touching these topics! I defend: here I am, physical and alienated. Here is my interior world, my love and anger. Here are the joy husks that might still hold a seed. Surely I'm not prevented from scripting my own sacrednesses? I went home, talked to people whose support emphasized my "right" to free movement, free speech, who left me alone with my desire to listen. I'm not desperate to defend self-expression that disowns context, I say. Your approval, I tell defensive friends, isn't the deal. It's the blind privilege which I physically embodied where you expected empathy. I overstepped. I am skeptical of public remorse missives; there are templates now for "real" apologies that anyone with some public relations smarts can replicate according to their gaffe. The world feels frantic-mad with ever more unrest; my thoughts and my discourse remain unsettled, meaning to, meaning to sound empathies that unsettle fairness-as-white and interrogate Canadian idiom's distance from the truth. From advantage, ignorantly, I've expressed furors I haven't fought for. This text won't earn trust that isn't there. That's fair. If I've learned, it will show outside the page's white, beyond the media's bright light. I turn with open heart toward your story:

149

His home is white privilege. I've retreated into an easygoingness that holds itself above the perturbations of racism or poverty. He reads news stories about appropriations which have no correspondence with the routines of his bright Victoria fatherhood and respectability. We have sex and breakfast. Where is my judgment fled, that ensconces me snugly here, in this bubble of false tranquility? What right do I have to enjoy it? He has responsibilities: a reno, dog, kids on weeknights, emails, briefs to write. He has a taste for organic beef, fair trade coffee, the world's harshness filtered into an economy that fails others, somewhere, far away. He's doting, clean-cut, punctual, so what if he makes mean jokes about trashy clothes or watching corpulent men dominate me? I don't want to say this attention is not welcome. So satisfied, this way of being, so perfect. If I'd just lighten up, I could be loved. If I could just roll with winky tells of his desire for student-prof naughty time. He almost loves me: why else would he listen to my stories of past repulsive abuse, all the men who've dishonoured me, without wincing? The man listens, unmoving, without a twitch, and says unh-hunh. At local events we play count the brown people (three in two hundred)—it's edgy chat; it's an amuse-bouche. I decide not to be vexed with watching gala auctions or bring down with tears another marvellous invitation to shower. Why don't I meet the kids? Would I greet his mom? I'm ecstatic at his kisses; I moderate my views. To me, he's unbelievable: a listener-lover-friend, who sees me? At the brunch spot with cilantro-and-lime crème fraîche, he happily lives, insouciant. Like life on Mars, my life, to him—but he loves sci-fi; it's fun imagining other worlds. It's over, I say with tears. This poem is now just keeping me busy as I try to make blind senseless shit into poetry. He was warm and gentle. Intelligent and sweet-smelling. The boyfriend I should have gotten over before assault whispered what I should find a comfort.

My body is so bomb I can't stand it. Holy hustler of curves, holy butter of cocoa, loves, I am royal. I have to lie down, loves, in the revving of this whorl, this energic gliss of rubbing against myself with lithe penis or party toy. Spanked by fortune, I'm sort of not-he, wethot pink-brown at the dew hole, grinding fortune's gotchas into the yum of myself. This gymnastic flexibility grants, unfolds, grants. Physically young-lady-like, with sophisticated fetish kinaesthetics, I bend into that thing I do. They call me baby, or girlfriend, or Sonnet, but whole is my word for my own state; they enjoy a succulence that I body beyond who wolves or fawns upon it. Oh na na, my fit is so fit I have to ooh, mon cul, si doux—I rise into unashamedness, groan into touchscape, undo the retributions venged upon myself. With repaired consent I moan my sweetheart merit. I drip, soaking in my own self-respect. This animate isness, so proud that its happy survives, survives and cries out throated pleasures. A penis is isness . . . when I can't swallow masculinity I'm still bedheaded, still laid into the worship of this bodily god-reflection. I command my own erection; I'm rivered by the motion of my touch, silkening inside. My eyes are beauty beholders, loves. Haters gonna hate. This hot form knows itself unbroken, now; this hot body cleared its mind. Those old traumas that the eye can't see, I come through them. I let go—of narratives—into a nerved exaltation; my diamond-Black wholeness shines and shines.

O! from what power the rapist wants his sorry to be enough. The rapist's powerful friends, mighty with representation, ink a suffering conscience their way. They want to muzzle my heart, to sway my stand, to make me give their lies grace, gaslight my own true sight, and swear that their brothering hasn't enabled their brother's sadistic offsides. It's his birthday —come on, you won't disgrace the day with old offences, when he wants to throw us all this party? say brothers and their groomed companions. Speaking of offensive things makes us ill, stirs hatreds in the family's covert psyche: we refuse confrontation with buddy's deeds, when there is such strength in our propaganda. Meanwhile, the scared rapist can't exorcise the spectre of his act. He'd kill the account—that's all in my mind—by threatening my mind's worth. His unaccountability depends on fellow bullies' tacit sexcapade endorsement and bitches like me who've been taught to heel. He wonders how to make me love him—love, the most effective mollifier. Love, that tenders the most reconciliatory heart. Can't my hard eyes see his remorse? Are bygones just cause of hate? Meanwhile, I've got to hold a job while I ugh his love delusion, while his associated brothers doorkeep. If I work with his brothers (and who aren't his brothers?), am I disgusting? Should I disgust myself, for not abhorring their money and state? I feel my filthy unworthiness every day, that I pay my bills without decolonizing everything that touches me. #metoo, write workers-through-the-mindfuck-of-property. We will be untroubled only where we know ourselves, beloved, of the earth.

Look, everything is fire. You're not too young to know why caution is, to know how its conscience hides the baby from the predator, protects the littles who know no self-protection, but your tinder conscience is my iron womb, in filings. Stillborn, it is the ferrous flint of everything, it is fire, now buried in the gentlemanned soil. You'll true cheaters with sass, urgent one? You didn't invent mouthy. I am dry lips; I suckled star-starved, guilty ogre-fathers. My faultlines and my earthy soil, my sweet wet seasons of earnest flirtation, done been inflamed: a coal pair of ovaries hang from the heartgash. Ideologues, betrayers of kingdom, everything is fire. Fierce daughters seize the robes and silver tray; money moves in nanoscopic, bloodborne binary floods; corporate partners yeah-yeah to mommy's gross purpose, her body's foetal reason. My soul's been a dothead, marked with ashes; my soul's been a Black woman Christianly offering her body. It's been our hearts, terrified, as he finishes. Maybe fire will triumph, and be everything. Look, everything, our flesh, is so lit right now, it says one word and Holy Fuck. Sparks tongue the dry forest, looking for a soothing lick or sick burn. Pricks, used to rising at the please-eyes of unnamed subordinates, have their swollen heads pointed out—they feel as if minions hoist red pitchforks. Social justice martyrs pass torches to kids who want to light up old bros' clubs til they blaze. But good men are proud of their patriarchies' paternal side. The truth, the truth, the truth is on fire; we just want our content let the dream of progress burn! This year, in the province, forty-five thousand were evacuated—the ragiest season ever, say B.C. wildfire information officers. How is Environment Canada handling its harassy bosses and internal affairs? Burning sky is falling. The boys of the Royal Canadian Mounted Police escort children to shelter; the women are entering eleven hundred official claims into class action suits. Fort Mac's resilience, TV beholds as if it staggers out of a hellfire apocalyptic; near Williams Lake, the Tsilhqot'in resilience sticks around. Everything is fire. Are you green, who speak like dropping a cigarette from a moving car, who flick explosive truth bombs at first responders? I still, when fury-green, spit gasoline on the tender flames of scared, self-sheltering souls.

In the body of a settler of colour. Living on the territory, here, of the Snuneymuxw. Knowing so little. I am the first coloured person to work in my department. About protocols, some white women instruct me. A starlet says, wouldn't it be nicer for a Snuneymuxw professor to have your institutional platform? I turn the question up loud, until it overspeaks every word of my bearing. Listen to it, you act of unsettled history. How do I be here, how don't I be, vowelling over British work, here, standing in classrooms, here, leaving the word faith to ring out in the voweling, or even saying Snuneymuxw, here? Latecomer, fragile af, say the ringers. White men in my classroom have been learning Hul'q'umi'num' verbs in Duncan. Tfw they really listen to a non-white body. So unfamiliar. Then tfw the Woke Police lay trumped-up charges on my (I can't) breath(e). When yuh changin steady and yuh lookin fancy, my mom calls out, dey goin to say that yuh showin off. Yes, Mom, but they call it critique, and when I break they tweet that I'm no aunty. I am performing injury for demonstrative purposes, says this performance of language. All my vowels are throated hellos to you, speaker, be you traumatized or misusing every privilege that you seized from capital. And all my honest faith informs the consonance I mean to sew. Lots of shitty, self-absorbed "allies" have sworn deep oaths of empathy and aims of deep kindness, Sonnet. I oath only that I am soft and thirsty for love, that my truth still searches for its home-body on decolonial horizons. That to train me in complacency, Canada promised to enlighten me, then they gave white boys the gigs of experts-in-Black-poetries. I stand in front of teens, but the lesson is Robinson's, or Maracle's, or Deerchild's; the room is on Snuneymuxw territory. I'll mark arguments arguing they understand the things the writers see, when arguably their silences are more informed than me. I live on Snuneymuxw territory, on Douglas Treaty unfinished business, near foreshore on which the Port Authority projects, where four Chinatowns' memories were disappeared. You just got hired so the institution can swear it's not racist, say anonymous eggs. I can't tell if they're nationalists, hating the affront of my Black authority, or my ally sisters, unsoftened by a dougla Douglas displays to protect himself.

Cusp of liquid allah, liquid body of this body, you understand. I'm an island, fracture of terrestrial biologics, animals and lake esophageals, mountain and soilfield intestinals. The humans I flower through are islands, conceiving in a Christened time. My age, pre-Pacific, you understand. Birth is your flowing, your wave-kindling. Your pointed firs grow seagreen and liquid in round quickenings. Liquid body, steeling a Pacific name, coldly intuitive, you ally my injury. Ocean, you ally fountains of thoughtful animality, you blueground the wind. You rush in like a paramedic, shouldering, bodying sorrow's speed from the moon. You rush in, shouldering a jellyfishy humour, reminding me of love. I am dateless and alive, like you. I'm finished being alone in this terrestrial longing. What we have to endure, we have, to endure. It's been grief, all along—you knew that. You see me, continental gentleness, black basalt bathwater, awash with thrown babies. They were children, of the colony, who foretold I would never mother their kind. I proved shitty as aggrocultured, Canadian soil: I was fragrant, strong, and germinating all kinds of planets; I was worldliness and sovereign. They could not breed their polite brutality at my breast; I would not make kids for any country unequal to me. The colony came dressed as boyfriends, trading Love for my subordination. I wanted a partner in work and fairness, a world-father, boyful, for the realization of a child's need, whose lips would touch my breast knowing desire sucks at seas within, and bring himself, imperfect and humble, to help me grow oceans. Safely. Bathed in desire because I am body, vaginal ground to salt sea, I sheltered my birthmothering through cities and jobs, across land distempered, guest everywhere but my own solitude. I found no country where the baby could come. Now my gutflower, flesh jellyfish, is buried in Okanagan's missioned territory, wherever the hospital disposes of anomalies. And where you cusp, liquid godness, I am relation. I am home with your green firs. I exhume my mum dream from colonial amnesias. Its uterine leather, I wash in your seagreen personhood, raise it full of memory, and sip.

The little love bud God gave them, virgins, after lying together once, was me. Immaculate-ish conception in Tkaronto. Would you like to abort it? the doctor lullabyed. Was this my first brush with death-by-racism? My mother didn't have to be Christian to flame in gobsmacked anger and decline to whisk away the little guestimate noobying in her tummy. Then the seemly priest who was to hear their vows pulled Dad aside to chasten him—it's your life, you don't have to keep careless promises to marginal people—encouraging him to back away from us. But a la entwined her maiden hand and his together, or Fate did, and the rest is my devotional history. Creation took up their names. The fusion of their cells was alphabetically echoed in my name: s-o-n from Jason—onomastic dicotyledons, genesis coded—and n-e-t from Janet, make s-o-n-n-e-t. Foundational metaphor, jeux de mots at the heart of "me," foreshadowing a wordy mind and a sonnet's heart-led, argumentative nature. A handle glorifying rhyme, song, and meter, derived at the intersectionality of cultures, a weave of ancestors, double-eponymed. I'm languaged by waves of colonial converging, on stolen land, mothered and fathered into verse, armed with this brown hand. Shakespeare answered the question I ached in a prairie schoolyard: what am I? No Michelle or Brittany, me, who lived in disgrace with Fortune, whose melanin overspoke my friendly overtures. I took shelter from "what are you?", perpetuated by little growing babes, amidst the anguished iambs Shakespeare blueprinted. Hopeful, I read my name in respected rhythms. Fateful, for I never meant to endure in verse. Yeah, I've survived breeding outside matrimony's missions, but that priest's disciples got my children. Sacrificial, sullen, I came to this name's prophecy: for my children, this procedure. What contact languaged this body? It's something earthen I prove, plowing under verse familiar. Reeds of Shakespeare, tails of weather, soilfully I weave together. The coolie kids don't know which line to love.

Christina Sharpe's concepts of wake and weather, from *In the Wake: On Blackness and Being,* inform my sense of temporality. Marlene NourbeSe Philip's articulation of English as a foreign language, a foreign anguish, in *She Tries Her Tongue, Her Silence Softly Breaks,* and her careful engagement with erasure as well as her care to absolve herself of authorial intention in *Zong!* inform my approach to authorship. Frantz Fanon's ideas around overcoming psychological colonization informed the invention of the overwriting procedure, and the writings of Gloria Anzaldúa, Homi Bhabha, and Larissa Lai on subjectivity inform my inhabitation of "I." My representations of speaking and animate plants, water, and rocks are my own: I have written academically about the erasure, suppression, and poeticization of concepts of plant sentience in English literature. Leanne Betasamosake Simpson's care, in *Dancing on Our Turtle's Back,* around ensuring that Nishnaabeg concepts she encountered at a distance resonated within her own web of relationships, Chelsea Vowel's thoughts on the relationship possibilities of Indigenous language education for non-Indigenous peoples, and personal conversations all inform the representation of my contact with Indigenous knowledges.

LXXXIV—LXXXVIII: When considering reiterating the Truth and Reconciliation Commission of Canada's 94 *Calls to Action,* I was guided by the commission's indication that "anyone may, without charge or request for permission, reproduce all or part" of its 2015 report. In the poems, I follow the language of the report in my use of the word *Aboriginal.* Mindful of Greg Younging's style recommendations around this term, however, I have also used the word *Indigenous* as much as possible.

XCII and CI: Names and identifying details have been changed.

Earlier versions of many of these poems originally appeared in various online and print magazines and anthologies. Many thanks to all the editors of the following publications who solicited and/or published this work. "I," "II," "III," and "IV" appeared in *The Goose,* Summer 2012. "V" appeared in *The Poetry Review* (UK), Winter 2012. "VI" appeared in *Canadian Poetries*, November 2012. "VII" and "XI" appeared in *Canada and Beyond*, Volume 3, 2013. "VIII" and "XI" appeared in *filling Station*'s Experimental Women Writers issue, 2013. "X" appeared in *This Magazine*, November/December 2014. "XII," "XVII," "XXI," "XXVI," and "XL" appeared in *TRUCK*, February 21, 2015. "XIII" appeared in *The Capilano Review*'s *ti-TCR* 9, 2014. "XIV," "XV," "XVI," and "XXXVI" appeared in *N/A Lit Journal*, June 2015. "XVIII" appeared in *The Cordite Poetry Review* (Australia), December 1, 2014. "XIX" and "XX" appeared in *newpoetry. ca*, August 21, 2014. "XXII" appeared in *lemonhound.com*, August 25, 2014. "XXIII," "XXIV," and "XXV" appeared in *ISLE: Interdisciplinary Studies in Literature and Environment* 24:4, December 2017. "XXIII," "XXXIII," and "LVII" appeared in *Best American Experimental Writing 2016*, edited by Seth Abramson and Jesse Damiani. "XXVII" and "XXXV" appeared in *The New Quarterly* Issue 134, Spring 2015. "XXVIII" and "XXIX" appeared in the *Partisan*'s "The Pitch Series" in January 2016. "XXX" appeared in *Poetry Is Dead Magazine*'s Work Issue, 2015. "XXXI," "XLI," and "XLII" appeared in *Drunken Boat*, February 6, 2017. "XXXII," "LIII," and "LXI" appeared in *Tripwire 12*. "XXXIII" appears in *The Revolving City: 51 Poems and the Stories Behind Them*, edited by Wayde Compton and Renée Sarojini Saklikar. "XXXIV" appeared in *Delirious Hem* in November 2014. "XXXVII" and "XXXVIII" were commissioned by *The Walrus Talks* for its philanthropy-themed event in Toronto on December 5, 2015. "XXXIX," "LXXII," and "LXVIII" appeared in *Numéro Cinq*, October 2016. "XLIII," "XLIV," and "XLVI" appeared in *Touch the Donkey*, January 2016. "XLV" appeared in *Vallum*. "XLVIII" and "L" will appear in *Harriet's Legacies: Race, Historical Memory and Futures in Canada*, edited by Natalee Caple and Ronald Cummings. "XLIX," "LIV," "XCII," and "CV" appeared in *The Capilano Review*, Summer 2017. "LVI" and "LVII" were published as a broadside by No Press, July 2015. "LVIII," "LIX," "LXII," and "LXIV" appeared in *Room Magazine*'s Women of Colour issue 39:1. "LX" appeared in *Dusie*, August 9, 2016. "LXVIII" appears in *Resistance*, an anthology on sexual assault edited by Sue Goyette. "LXX," "LXXI," and "XCV" appeared in *The Fiddlehead* 270, Winter 2017. Very early versions of "LXXIII" and "LXXXV" appeared in *TRUCK*, August 19, 2012. "LXXIV," "LXXV," and "LXXVII" appeared in *The Rusty Toque*. "LXXIX" and

"CXXXV" appeared in *lemonhound 3.0,* October 10, 2017 and in 2019 "LXXIX" was chosen to appear in an anthology of selections from Lemon Hound online magazine. "LXXXI" appeared in *The Goose* 14.2. "LXXXIV," "LXXXV," "LXXXVI," "LXXXVII," and "LXXXVIII" appeared in *Canadian Literature* 230-231 (Autumn/Winter 2016). "LXXXIX" and "XC" appeared in *White Wall Review* 41 (2017). "XCI" appears in *GUSH: Menstrual Manifestos for Our Times,* edited by Roseanna Deerchild, Ariel Gordon, and Tanis MacDonald. "LCIV" appears in *Refugium: Poems for the Pacific,* edited by Yvonne Blomer. "XCVI" and "XCVII" appeared in *Intercapillary Space,* December 2016. "XCVIII," "CI," and "CII" appeared in *PRISM international* 55:3, Spring 2017. "CI" was also chosen by Hoa Nguyen to appear in *Best Canadian Poetry in English, 2018.* "CIV," "CXI," "CXXVII," and "CXXXI" appeared in *The Capilano Review*'s "Work of Words" issue, Winter 2018. "CXXVII" was also chosen by Rob Taylor for inclusion in *Best Canadian Poetry 2019.* "CVIII" appeared in *The Town Crier/Puritan Magazine,* March 24, 2017. "CXII," "CXXXIX," and "CL" appear in *Refuse: CanLit in Ruins,* edited by Hannah McGregor, Julie Rak, and Erin Wunker. "CXIII" appeared in *This Magazine,* Jan-Feb 2018. "LXIII," "CIII," "CIV," and "CVII" appeared in *poemeleon*'s Canadian issue, edited by rob mclennan. "CXIV" was published in *Poetry Magazine,* December 2017, and discussed in *The Poetry Magazine Podcast* for that month. "CXXIV" appears in the essay "Tree, I Invented a New Form of Poem" on *poetryfoundation.org.* "CXXVIII" was commissioned by the Nanaimo Art Gallery for the *Dream Islands* exhibit, Summer 2017, and was published in collaboration with The Blasted Tree as a limited-edition broadside. "CXXVIII" also appears in *The Next Wave: An Anthology of 21ˢᵗ Century Canadian Poetry,* edited by Jim Johnstone. "CXLVII" appears in *Vallum,* Spring 2019.

ACKNOWLEDGEMENTS

This book was written with the support of a Canada Council Grant for Professional Writers.

Thank you to all the friends and acquaintances who gave me their permission to be named in these poems, and to Phedra for her permission regarding the girls.

Thank you to Dionne Brand: "Poetry is here, just *here*. Something wrestling with how we live, something dangerous, something honest."

Thanks many times over to Jared and Kelly at McClelland & Stewart.

Thanks to Molly Peacock, Tanis MacDonald, Erin Moure, Carmine Starnino, George Murray, Derek Beaulieu, and Lee Ann Brown, who showed interest in and support of this project in its earliest stages. To Carmine again and Simon Dardick for their kindness and encouragement through difficulties. Also to Carleton Wilson and rob mclennan for their enthusiasm. Larissa Lai and Ashok Mathur, thank you for your mentorship. Thanks to Fred Wah and Pauline Butling, West Coast poetic elders, and to everyone in A Drift Collective for conversations. To Erin Wunker, Natalee Caple, Jacqueline Valencia, Priscila Uppal, Soraya Peerbaye, Anita Lahey, Daniel Zomparelli, and Sachiko Murakami, I am grateful for conversations around writing in community. Interactions with Elee Kraljii Gardiner, Lucia Lorenzi, Gillian Jerome, Amber Dawn, Nilofar Shidmehr, Vivek Shraya, Paul Vermeersch, Bianca Spence, Elisabeth de Mariaffi, Rita Wong, Stephen Collis, Emily Nilsen, and Jónína Kirton helped me continue this work when it got hard.

Priscila, I carry with me always the memory of your enthusiasm for life, for friendship and for finished projects. I raise a glass of prosecco to you, friend.

Thanks to Délani Valin for her work on the manuscript and for saying the struggle is real.

Thank you to Katherena Vermette for comments on a few poems that affected my approach to the whole book.

Thanks to Lee Ann Brown for organizing readings of this work at Cambridge University and in Brighton, U.K. Thanks Ghazal Mosadeq for the reading and hospitality in London, to Jonathan Skinner for the panel at AWP in Washington, D.C., and to Alessandro Porco, also for Washington's AWP and for the reading at University of North Carolina —Wilmington. Thanks Madhur Anand for the reading in New York. Don Share at *Poetry*, thanks for your enthusiasm for these poems well before one of them appeared in your magazine.

Thanks to my former and present colleagues and students at University of British Columbia—Okanagan, at Wilfrid Laurier University, and Vancouver Island University.

Thanks to Court, Crystal, Teresa, Paul, and Priscila for invaluable friendship. Cynthea, Nicole, Melissa, and Farah, let's hang out soon.

Jordan and Tan, Mila and Giselle: View halloo!

Dad, thank you for showing me we can transform the fatherhoods we inherit. Mom, I was only able to write this because I am your daughter. The two of you—your affection, the stories of reactions to you as a couple, your struggles and artistic ideals—were my first country. I love you both.

INDEX OF ENTRY POINTS

1   seed, where are you from?

2   so gazed on in kelowna

3   wickaninnish

4   lace-edged leg holes of identity

5   vancity like he owned

7   words so profuse

8   the steep funnelling steps

9   sound your last zeptosecond

10 wetness blipped from supernovas'

11 relationship need

12 are these my fathers

13 i'll grope what i want

14 knitty nodules of power blanketry

15 being with your rock

16 dermal tint

17 you, bro

18 touched as earthly fetish

19 between the bard's consonants

20 its levers, alive above

21 material fantasies

22 devotional whinery of unfair

23 attend to sisters

24 duckfaces over record temperatures

25 promiscuous open mining

26 maybe northern seas

27 strong libido

28 hunts, languaging, chastening

29 your witch's spelled wrong

30 now happiness opens

31 all those grievances forgone

32 ivory towers

33 clades

34 soundclouds float above transit

35   campus shenanigans

36   limned in vedas

37   shots heard in ottawa

38   benefactor

39   to give a shit

40   christmas loneliness

41   la marseillaise moves

42   seize terror's media

43   shakespeare, i confront

44   mobilized in lined eyes

45   digitally held tender flows

46   my unliterary shrill

47   university humanists

48   breakfast turns into us

49   black when walking

50   tanya tagaq

51   your writings

52   hustlers

53   the unyearning set

54   describe no addictions

55   sweaters and apartments

56   priscila

57   sweet talker

58   unassuming bars of #d8dfea

59   let that shit go

60   aromatherapies

61   local ikeas

62   hoping you will facetime

63   administered formally by ryerson

64   the system that milks

65   only-minority-in-the-room

66   squats

67   if desdemona had

68   freshly assaulted

69   procrastinating

70   djadja

71 fictions of welcome

72 child on the sand

73 riot grrrls'

74 a superlative idealism

75 dope theatre

76 a space so vulnerable

77 the round table

78 the flip that breaks the internet

79 justin

80 urban dictionary

81 young feminist assholes

82 weathers the racial real

83 acupuncture

84 sexed with plants

85 calls 1-17

86 calls 18-42

87 calls 43-59

88 calls 60-76

89 calls 77-94

90 raised on fairy tales

91 bought a house

92 in red-soaked garments

93 pushing to adopt

94 bowie

95 west coast earthquake

96 phytotherapeutic woods

97 the minecrafty feminine

98 aww imagery

99 looking for someone

100 the first story i want

101 hillary clinton

102 just can't. i make excuses

103 the neurons firing

104 you're listening

105 a mauver level

106 ptsd-ing un mixed-up

107 pinks and light greens
108 next best president
109 fake poetry
110 bulbasaur's morph to ivysaur
111 the brown dog who tried
112 bouncing yuh backside
113 so manly
114 quietly, coral reefs
115 the land underfoot said
116 organize a thing
117 we marched
118 hallelujah
119 sublime, that magnificent blackness
120 vibrators, handles
121 a question of power
122 deity's declensions
123 tablespoons of sugar
124 to distinguish the eunoia
125 what happened was rape
126 winsome sister
127 bodies, phytosentient
128 you see yourself profaned
129 pots' forms like performances
130 ethical diamond leader
131 my muse
132 my game
133 smallest homegirl
134 articles that mention wikipedia
135 simpson's books
136 when i'm stoned
137 mansion or crack house
139 an ethos. overachiever
140 brit in the woodpile
141 don't call me bystander
142 don't read the comments
143 plastic gulls water

165

144   inkside of your body

145   boy-next-door

146   raccoon nation

147   granmudda way

148   this new person is my boyfriend

149   free speech

150   life on mars

151   my own erection

152   it's his birthday—come on

153   the ragiest season

154   settler of colour

155   liquid allah

156   this name's prophecy

SONNET L'ABBÉ is the author of two previous collections of poetry, *A Strange Relief* and *Killarnoe*, and, most recently, the chapbook *Anima Canadensis*, which won the 2017 bpNichol Chapbook Award. In 2000, she won the Bronwen Wallace Memorial Award for most promising writer under thirty-five. In 2014, she was the guest editor of *Best Canadian Poetry in English*. Her work has been internationally published and anthologized. L'Abbé lives on Vancouver Island and is a professor of creative writing and English Literature at Vancouver Island University.